The Magic of Caithness

Published by

NORTH OF SCOTLAND NEWSPAPERS

© Copyright 1998 North of Scotland Newspapers. All Rights Reserved.

A catalogue record for this book is available from the British Library.

ISBN 1 871704 22 7

Typeset by North of Scotland Newspapers,
42 Union Street, Wick, Caithness, Scotland.
Printed by Highland Printers, Henderson Road, Inverness, Scotland.
Cover Illustration – Designsmith.

"Old Herring Drifters in Wick Bay"
Photographed by Dan Mackay

The Magic of Caithness

Edited by
RONALD THOMSON

Published by

NORTH OF SCOTLAND NEWSPAPERS,
42 UNION STREET, WICK, CAITHNESS, SCOTLAND

THE MAGIC OF CAITHNESS

Affectionately dedicated to Mother
who introduced us to the land of her
forebears – Caithness. Also in memory
of my twin brother Alan: man of many
talents.

This is the magic and mystery of Caithness –
To come upon the hidden, the untold
and unknown discoveries on our own doorstep.

Dan Mackay

FOREWORD

I was not blessed with the experience of a childhood in Caithness, but at least had the privilege of spending my summer holidays there in my childhood in the 1940s. The paternal side of my family was Caithnessian and even my mother's side sprang from the nearby Ross and Cromarty – almost a bordering county. Because of my uncle, Neil Gunn, the famous Scottish novelist, I was steeped in Highland folklore and particularly that pertaining to Caithness. Caithness was part of me and remains part of me. It is an integral part of the Scotland I love, both past and present.

In one of the many exciting contributions to this wonderful collection of poetry and prose dedicated to Caithness, Scotland's nothernmost county on the mainland, a question is posed: "Is there anything north of Inverness?" Sadly, I have heard this query in the company of many tourists of goodwill from England, the Continent and America. It echoes in its structure the more profound question about life after death. Strangely enough, the answers to both the terrestrial and spiritual questions are answered, possibly obliquely, by the contributors to this splendid collection of poetry and prose.

All the contributors have connections with Caithness. Some live there; others are exiles and some are outsiders who have fallen in love with the county. Some are alive; others are dead. I have to say that I experience a sense of guilt in being a Gunn in exile in Edinburgh. Comfort comes from Rousseau, the great French writer, who maintained that a writer wrote better about summer when enduring the hardships of winter and about winter when basking in summer sunshine. The Russian Turgenev wrote about his beloved country – its birch woods, its endless plains and its enchanting women when living in voluntary exile in France. Fair France, with all its charm, could not obliterate the memories of his native Russia. Humbly, I share their views.

It is difficult to disentangle time from place. My uncle, Neil Gunn, came nearest to this synthesis of time and place in his novel "Sun Circle", a novel concerning the genesis of Caithness – a mixing of Picts, Celts and Norse people to form a new race to inhabit an old land. The mix of Celtic and Nordic place names bear witness to this tempestuous beginning. Elsewhere Gunn was to write in an essay on the north on the approach to Caithness from over the Ord, the dividing line on the East between Sutherlandshire and Caithness: "From that background, or as it were from that door, you walk out upon Caithness and at once experience an austerity in the flat, clean, wind-swept lands that affect the mind almost with a sense of shock. There is something more in it than contrast. It is a movement of the spirit that finds in the austerity, because strength is there also, a final serenity. I know of no other landscape in Scotland that achieves this harmony, that in the very moment of purging the mind of its dramatic grandeur, leaves it free and ennobled. The Pentland Firth, outreaching on the left, is of a blueness that I, at least, failed to find in the Mediterranean; a living blueness, cold glittering in the sun and smashed to gleaming snowdrift on the great rock battleships of the Orkneys, bare and austere also. The winds of time had searched out even the flaws here and cleansed them." In this paragraph pregnant with meaning, Gunn is crossing one boundary from the South and referring to another boundary, a watery one, the Pentland Firth that distances Caithness from the Northern Isles. Both boundaries are dramatic in their texture. The sentinels in the South are the "magical mountains" – I can find no other epithet – of Morven, the Maiden Pap and Scaraben – and in the North the ice-blue sea, the

"Sunset over Dunnet Head"
Photographed by Ronald Thomson

stacks and the islands of Orkney. Morven, the Maiden Pap and Scaraben are exceptions, for Caithness is a vast plain and its very flatness emphasises the feeling of light and space. The feminine land is sister to the masculine sea and both are in communication with a changeable sky. This feeling is echoed in the contributions to this remarkable collection – a collection that reminds the reader that amidst the elemental facets of land, sea and sky, there are the sheltered straths where the little burn and the wild flower are predominant. I quote from three poems in the anthology that juxtapose the great and small. The first two emphasise the great and the elemental.

> "Bold is the Caithness sea
> Alive with a zest for life,
> By rock, cliff or goe,
> Fresh as the caller wind"   **[Caithness Sea]**

and

> "My song shrieks hard on the gale:
> I know the unriven rock
> Yet when my young ones call
> I turn, I am"   **[The Seagull]**

The third poem is quiet and intimate

> "Bright berried rowans,
> Foxgloves in ranks,
> Noisy burns rushing
> Twixt primrose-starred banks"   **[Memory Pictures]**

From place to time. The anthology deals most adequately with the passage of time in Caithness from the Viking invasions to the development of Dounreay. Everything is cyclic, and Caithness at the periphery of mainstream developments mirrors many of them. The preparation for the Battle of Largs against a Scottish King, the struggle for the Earldom of Caithness, the clearances in the late 18th and early 19th century and the herring boom of the 19th century. The last-mentioned event brought in money, people and an awareness of what this county means to Scotland and the United Kingdom. Among the distinguished visitors were Robert Louis Stevenson, Hugh Miller and later Lord Kitchener and Harold MacMillan. In the 19th century the continentals used to describe Britain as a coal field surrounded by fish.

There was a strong element of truth in this description and Caithness certainly appreciated that its comparative affluence depended on fish. Fishing villages appeared at river estuaries and even a railway was built to connect Lybster, a prominent fishing village, to Wick, the fishing capital of the north. It was an exciting period, but it had passed.

What remains? On this point the collection is reassuring. The poetry is not always nostalgic, although the past is often the compost for a positive move into the future. The characters portrayed in the collection are fascinating in their diversity and attributes. The work of such wonderful chroniclers of Caithness as Calder and Horne have been brought to the attention of the reader. What a debt we owe to them and what a starting point their example can give to us now!

It would be invidious for me to single out any particular contribution for attention or praise. All are of the highest order, marshalled and placed with loving care by Ronald Thomson. One contribution, however, captured my imagination. It concerned a scenario for "Alice in Wonderland" in Caithness. There is nothing absurd about this as youth is always at the heart of things, even in such areas as diverse as Oxfordshire and Caithness. The essay reminds me of a lovely passage in Neil Gunn's "Morning Tide" concerning youth, a book that embraces the wonder of the winds, tides and spates of rivers and burns. It concerns a little boy on a beach, who almost regards the sea as something animate. "Below the high tidal sweep of tangleweed the beach sloped in clean grey stones rounded and smooth, some no bigger than his fist. As he stepped on them they slithered and rolled with a sea noise. The noise rose up and roared upon the dusk like a wave. All around there was no life to be seen, there was no movement but the sea's."

It would be misleading to end this foreword without mention of the county's two fine towns of Wick and Thurso. Their history reflects the history of the county in good and bad times. Both are memorials to certain periods in the county's history. Both are centres of education, culture and commerce. The healthy rivalry between the two ensures a standard of excellence in the quality of life in a part of Scotland that differs from all the other counties that form the Kingdom of Scotland. The phrase "Over the Ord" will always maintain its overtones or undertones of magic. This book, a rich mosaic of time, place and feeling, will help both native and visitor to fall under the spell of a very special "plot" of land.

Dairmid Gunn
Edinburgh, May, 1995.

CATANASIA

*(The ancient name given to our county on a very old map and inspiring
these verses upon our long heritage)*

Northland, whose steep cliffs scaured and majestic,
    Reach out to meet a deep rolling sea,
Down to the tide where white foam aswirling
    Washes the rocks, relentless and free.

Stately they curve the wild rocky headlands
    Out round the shore of our native home
With stacks out like bastions, the ramparts defending
    Or, as sentinels, watching where fishermen roam.

For there far below, lie the goes and the harbours
    Where safely they steer their barks to the shore,
With the white wings of "scorries" following after
    Screaming, and ready to snatch from the shore.

As high on the wind, round the time weathered clett rocks,
    The seabirds are calling, so eerie to hear,
Resounding in echo, where dark caves are lurking
    The hiding, where seals make their home without fear.

Yet tranquil the scene on a bright summer morning,
    When crystals are dancing far out on the sea,
With the breeze in the gorse on the green crested summits,
    And the cattle are browsing about on the lea.

Out on the lea to the purple clad moorland,
    Land of horizons and far distant view,
To the mountains that rise in solitude's silence,
    This the long vision our forefathers knew.

So to our heritage, ancient in story,
    Where stand the proud castles around our fair land,
For the home is the castle where peat reek unfurls
    <u>Catanasia,</u> forever, beloved and grand.

Jessie G. McLeod.

BEYOND THE ORD

I got up on a morning dim like all the others,
But when I opened the door a warm air met me,
And skylarks were lettering the sky's blue missal with gold.

May had come. The wide moors still lay silent
Except for the lark-song and peewits. They will always be so!
Too many spirits haunt there for easy speaking.

Today the sea flung splendour.
Blue patches laced with the white of foam
Advanced to the rocks, withdrew, advanced, like shawls

Held by a dancer high above her head:
Her elbow is the rock, so secretly lichened,
Only I, who have sat there, lived there, know the language.

The high fields, and the marshes
Where the coltsfoot gleamed, and now the ladysmock,
And irises creeping bright yellow,

Line the road. The old mill gazes
Down at the ruined harbour with gulls wheeling,
With oyster-catchers catching their own brief shadows.

The burn flows here, flows on for ever.
I close my eyes, and the sound is the answer to all things,
Beyond peace, beyond war.

Men have not listened to this sound
Or they would throw down their angry weapons and hear
The music that answers the burn-song.

Here it is summer, and Caithness leans alive
On the shoulder of eternity,
Dark moors are purple. Lochs like moonstones quiver

With ageless magic. Past weaves here with future.
Today is spun from a million delicate fabrics:
The sky is dancing.

Arthur Ball.

A great part of the magic of Caithness lies in the beauty of her coastline, for there are fine beaches and glorious cliff scenery. Take, for example, the cliffs at Holborn Head, who could fail to be impressed by them? Anyone familiar with the terrain will recall the De'il's Brig, the Clett-Rock, the amazing colonies of sea-birds wheeling and swooping against those mighty cliffs, while far below the sea ebbs and flows against the giant ramparts.

Sunset over Dunnet Head has a wonder of its own when the sea is aglow with light - a great path of gleaming, shimmering light, when fiery red has changed to gold; and this upon the very edge of mainland Scotland, without a whisper of wind. Memorable too is Dunnet Sands with the surf gently breaking on the shore with its own hypnotic beat, and all around there is a feeling of peace and tranquility.

Byron described the sea as "the image of eternity" in one of his classic poems[1], and there is a timeless allure about those elements which cover two-thirds of the world's surface. The people of Caithness are lucky to have so many fine beaches, so many grand cliff walks, so many vantage points to behold their wonderful and varied coastline. Many live their lives by the great restless sea, their crofts or farms are scattered along the northern seaboard. They who savour the salty taste of the sea and inhale the invigorating air of the Pentland Firth or North Sea, they above all, know a companion of infinite mood, a changing panorama of colours, an inspiration, a challenge, a natural force unharnessed by man.

[1] *Lord Byron: "Childe Harold's Pilgrimage".*

CHAPTER 1
THE GATEWAY TO CAITHNESS

Think of a triangle and you can imagine the shape of Caithness, for this "northern triangle" has its base in the hills, with the apex pointing to Norway.

The striking feature of Caithness is its flatness, its lack of hills and trees; it has little in common with Scotland from a geo-physical viewpoint; the county is smaller than its next door neighbour, Sutherland but is better populated.

Caithness has a coastline of 105 miles; bounded north by the Pentland Firth, east by the North Sea and south-east by the Moray Firth. The landward area consists of 685.7 square miles, plus the Island of Stroma.

For a long time Caithness was an "unknown" part of Scotland. Robert Louis Stevenson says in a notable essay (Random Memories – Education of an Engineer) that apart from sportsmen or antiquarians, no strangers visited the Far North. The exception, and it is a major one, was the influx of fisher folk to Wick during the herring season.

The most notable gateway to Caithness is via the east coast route where the road ascends to the Ord. The Ord is the boundary between Sutherland and Caithness – the name signifies "a steep hill or eminence" – it rises from sea level to 625 feet, and is $2\frac{1}{2}$ miles N.E. of Helmsdale, Sutherland.

This was a dangerous road in the old days, for the original route was little more than a path or shelf along the cliff edge, thus travellers alighted from horse or carriage. Unlike other Caithness headlands – which are mainly sandstone – the Ord is granite.

An ancient superstition which held it fatal for a Sinclair in green to cross the Ord on a Monday, relates to the massacre at Flodden (1513) when not one of 300 Sinclairs returned to Caithness.

There are miles of moorland north of the Ord and this wilderness continues until the road descends, dramatically, to the charming village of Berriedale, which is $7\frac{1}{2}$ miles north of Helmsdale.

There is a feeling of "sleepy hollow" about Berriedale, although it lies off the A9 road. Historian Calder (1794-1864) likened it to a beautiful Swiss scene in miniature, and it does have a distinctive appearance viewed from either side of the village.

The Langwell and Berriedale waters meet in this compact wooded village. The former rises from the wilds of Kildonan, the latter from the heights beyond Braemore. A timeless scene to watch the waters wend their way sea-ward and appreciate nature at work.

A fine War Memorial honours the fallen of two World Wars – a reminder that the preservation of freedom does not come without sacrifice:

> They shall grow not old, as we that are left grow old;
>   Age shall not weary them, nor the years condemn
> At the going down of the sun and in the morning
>   We will remember them[1].

Langwell House stands high above Berriedale, with one of the best views in Caithness. It was the summer residence of the late Duke of Portland. Langwell Estates have a long pedigree: Sir John Sinclair of Ulbster fame bought the estate in 1788 for £9,000 and sold it in 1811 for £40,000. A generation later it was bought by the Duke of Portland for £90,000, under whose ownership it became notable.[2]

A guest at Langwell was that veteran of the Sudan, Lord Kitchener. Herbert Sinclair in his fascinating picture-book "Caithness 1925-6" remembered Kitchener as an interested spectator at the Berriedale Games. Lord Kitchener it may be remembered, died in 1916 on board HMS Hampshire, off the Orkney coast en route for Russia, but that is another story.

Langwell Gardens are an oasis of colour in a county not famed for its climate, and a welcome surprise for the visitor. The great estates in Caithness have to contend with strong winds, and high walled gardens are a necessity for the rich variety of flowers and plants grown. The Gardens are usually open twice a year in aid of charity; visit them if you can.

There used to be a castle at Berriedale facing the sea – it was a stronghold of the Sutherland's of Langwell and Berriedale – the original Caithness castles were built by the Norsemen.

---

[1]*Laurence Binyon: For the Fallen.*
[2]*Prime Minister Harold MacMillan and his wife were guests at Langwell House in 1958.*

"Berriedale Shore"

Photographed by Dan Mackay.

Which traveller to Caithness does not remember the Berriedale Braes? This once "notorious" road notable for its steep gradient and hairpin bends has been much improved, but even today allows no room for complacency, and care must be the keynote.

On the way to Berriedale cove, a surprising discovery: grapes growing in a greenhouse! Something so far removed from the northern image can scarcely be imagined, yet there they grew, green grapes, a symbol of warmer climes.

The way to the pebble beach is via a narrow suspension footbridge, the kind which sways as you cross its path, while below, the vibrant river has almost reached "mecca" – the welcoming sea!

Standing in front of the disused houses by the fishing nets, one is reminded of an evocative heritage – the kind Neil Gunn reflected so well in novels like "Morning Tide" and "The Silver Darlings".

Those who wish to savour a distinctive part of Caithness might well visit Berriedale: what it lacks in size it compensates with character and a certain charm.

Between the Ord and Berriedale is the long deserted site of Badbea, which lies some 3 miles NE of the Ord facing the sea. As I descended the cliff and stood by the Cairn of Remembrance, a crow winged its way toward me like a sole guardian and croaked what seemed like a reproach.

Badbea came about as a result of the "Clearances" when families were left to eke a living from the very edge of the coastline – or emigrate. Caithness did not suffer on the scale of her neighbour, Sutherland, but it was bad enough.

I first read about Badbea many years ago but never imagined I would visit the site. It was like discovering a forgotten part of Caithness, a memorable experience, albeit a poignant one too.

The morning I journeyed to Badbea was perfect. After days of strong winds there was calm; where there had been rain and mist, there was sunshine and bright sky; the landscape was transformed and inviting.

Under the summer sun the sea was resplendent with alternating colours of blue and silver merging into infinity. Walking down the green sward which lies in front of the Cairn, it became easy to realise why young children had to be tethered lest they wander too near the cliff-edge.

Just outside one of the ruined crofts I was surprised to find a clump of rhubarb, and although the stalks were small they seemed healthy. Little remains of the Badbea which was a small community, for the stones of the dwellings are tumbled down covered with dead lichen. A sad reminder indeed.

The Cairn of Remembrance was erected in 1911 to commemorate the people of Badbea by David Sutherland of Wairappa and Wellington. Born in Badbea in 1806, he emigrated to New Zealand in 1839 and died there in 1877.

One name will always be linked with Badbea – that of John Sutherland or as he was better known: "John Badbea". He was born at Ousdale – not far from Badbea – in 1788. The families of Badbea knew him as a guiding light, he was in truth a patriarchal figure: kindly, humble and devout.

Rev. Alexander Auld records in his book: "Ministers and Men in the Far North" that John drew his strength from one source: "The love of Christ, which passeth all knowledge".

John Badbea died on 30th August, 1864, and was buried at Berriedale[1]. The Cairn of Remembrance at Badbea bears his name, and stands on the site of his former home.

By 1911 one person, John Gunn, remained at Badbea – the rest had emigrated: and for the exiles living in New Zealand, the words of Deuteronomy (chapter 8, verse 7) must have held special meaning:

"For the Lord thy God bringeth thee into a good land, a land of brooks of water, by fountains, and depths that spring out of hills".

A promised land indeed.

Few Caithness castles remain intact but among those which have survived is Dunbeath castle. In spring the driveway to the castle makes an appealing picture flanked by daffodils, this is prefaced by a tree-lined avenue which is attractive also.

The castle and grounds are not open to the public; however, once a year the Gardens are open in aid of charity. Dunbeath castle has been dated back to 1439, its most notable episode relates to the Marquis of Montrose's invasion of Caithness in 1650.

Montrose landed at Duncansby Head, with some two thousand men – he tried to recruit more for the Royalist cause in Thurso, but his appeal was almost ignored. In Orkney it had been a different story and many rallied to the call: but this northern invasion really began on the Continent with men and ships - the Prince of Orange supported the case of Charles II and supplied most of the vessels required by Montrose.

The news of Montrose's invasion "spread like wildfire" and Sir John Sinclair of Dunbeath castle set off for Edinburgh to summon help. Montrose in the meantime took possession of the castle without bloodshed and left a garrison there. This was intended as a place of refuge in case of any reverse in the Highlands.

[1]*The old burial ground is on the right hand side of the Berriedale Brae as you journey north. Giving a local man a lift in the car, I mentioned my visit to Badbea and John Badbea. "He was a good man - a holy man" he replied.*

Montrose instructed his brother to proceed south and raise more men; thus an advance party, some 500 in number, crossed into Sutherland. Now came the turning point against Montrose: General David Leslie headed north with 4,000 men plus an advance force of cavalry, and it was the latter who routed Montrose at Carbisdale, with a surprise attack.

Montrose escaped to Assynt in the wilds of Sutherland, where he wandered without food or shelter. He was caught by MacLeod of Assynt's men and taken to Ardvrack castle. No mercy was shown to Montrose and he was betrayed – for a price. Thus James Graham, Marquis of Montrose, was tried, condemned and executed, in the capital city of Edinburgh.

His brother was luckier: Captain William Gordon of Dunrobin, in pursuit of Henry Graham, arrived in Thurso a mite too late – for Graham aware of the Marquis's defeat – set sail from Scrabster to Orkney, and thence to Holland.

Driving south you can see Dunbeath castle facing the sea. It is a picturesque castle, white in colour, and from a distance suggestive of a castle from a children's picture-book.

Among the original inhabitants of Caithness were the Picts, whose era is probably the Bronze, or early Iron Age. They must have been resilient to wrest a living from such a primitive land as Caithness – barren windswept moorland for the most part, with a rough turbulent coast, yet perhaps the untamed suited their wild spirit?

One may only guess what motivated the Picts, for their lifestyle left no written record, save for those curious "symbol stones": some depict real objects, others abstract designs. The Ulbster stone is a notable reminder of their era.

Caithness is a land of standing stones and chambered tombs, but above all brochs – some 145 in number. Although generally described as "Pictish brochs" it is now believed that they belong to an earlier period:

"The excavations of some of the brochs yielded querns, weaving combs and spindles, as well as articles of personal adornment. These structures are referable to a period which must have extended over many centuries. The latest of them might have been in use when the Gaelic missionaries reached Caithness."

The brochs had a dual purpose: as dwellings and as defensive structures. Many were sited along the Caithness coast and up fertile straths. The broch remains an intriguing symbol of the Far North – one steeped in the mists of antiquity.

When the Norsemen invaded Caithness in the 9th century, the Celtic people were driven inland, thus the inheritors became the vanquished,

"Braemore" – the "Maiden Pap" (middle distance). *Photographed by Dan Mackay.*

and a new era began.

Vikings! The very name has a dramatic ring and finality: pagan and barbaric, they were remarkable seamen whose mastery of the sea remains unequalled for its time.

"The soul of the Vikings lay in the long-ship. They had evolved, and now, in the eighth and ninth centuries, carried to perfection, a vessel which by its shallow draught could sail in rivers, or anchor in innumerable creeks and bays, and which by its beautiful lines and suppleness of construction could ride out the fiercest storms of the Atlantic Ocean[1]."

Why those Scandinavian peoples – for the Vikings were not only Norwegian, but Swedish and Danish too – began their conquest of other lands is something for the historian to consider, suffice to say it marked an epoch in history.

Historian Calder says "Although Caithness had been long annexed, as a conquered province to the Norwegian rule in Orkney, it was never acknowledged as such by the Scottish monarchs; and nothing but its extreme distance from the seat of Government, the divided state of the kingdom, and the difficulty of sending troops far north and maintaining them there, forced them to tolerate usurpation."

Caithness was under Norse rule for nearly 400 years, yet strangely enough its influence appears to have been minimal regarding language, law or customs. Many place-names round the Caithness coast, however, are a reminder of the Norsemen.

The hamlet of Braemore is one of the loneliest places in Caithness. True it is only 6½ miles from Dunbeath, but the single track road draws the visitor to a Caithness Shangri-La, where the sense of isolation is strong.

The "Maiden Pap" (1,567 ft) overlooks this outpost of Caithness, which is border country. Where the road terminates there is the Berriedale water, some farmland, a plantation of trees and a phone box.

From Braemore Lodge, a private road leads to the only mountain in Caithness – Morven (2,313 ft) which is visible almost from one end of the county to the other. From Braemore it is 1½ hours brisk walking to the foot of Morven – the last stretch over boggy moorland.

Morven has a stark appearance close up, something raw and elemental in its massive frame. A novel experience to survey it at first

[1]*Winston S. Churchill: A History of the English Speaking Peoples (Vol. 1).*

In 1955, a Mr J. W. Mackay of Milton, Reay, discovered an ancient stone lamp while harrowing a field near his home. The lamp was believed to be almost 2000 years old, and examples of its kind have been found in brochs. (From Our Old Files: John O'Groat Journal).

hand, having seen it often frame the distant horizon with its neighbouring hills. When I climbed Morven, the weather was superb with only a little clouding at times.

I was alone on Morven, and the sense of solitude heightened as the landscape was deserted. Braemore seemed like an oasis on the horizon, with the "Maiden Pap" for company.

Who could forget the winding river snaking its way across the flat landscape - the river of life indeed. Someone like Thoreau might find solace in such a view, for he wrote: "My spirits infallibly rise in proportion to the outward dreariness. Give me the ocean, the desert, or the wilderness".

The north face is a steep climb and the summit deceptive – there are two peaks in fact. You may well rest on the first (an excellent view-point for a photograph) and survey the scene: eastward there are hills which contrast with Morven's lofty presence; westward the eye is drawn to a vast lunar-like landscape - primeval in character; northward – a reminder of civilisation, but above all a kingdom without players.

It's best to allow a full day if you intend to climb Morven, and wise to leave word, for this is an isolated area outwith the tourist zone. Caithness has a variable climate and is subject to strong winds, so like the Boy Scouts "be prepared"; also don't forget to bring refreshments – you'll need them!

Although I didn't set foot on the summit of Morven, I felt another Caithness ambition had been realised, almost in full. Things seen in retrospect leave their own impression, and the following poem (written on my return to Edinburgh) may speak for itself. One final thought with regard to mountain climbing: "festina lente" – hasten slowly.

MORVEN

Far beyond the wayward city
Beyond the path of men,
The river threads its way
Along the moorland plain,
Silver sunlight on the water
Bright against dark Morven.

Gone the winter snow
Which graced that mighty brow,
The icy winds which blew
From Ord to Dunnet Head,
Now unreserved sunshine
Warms the coldest heart.

Bone and sinew of Caithness
Yet unlike her in every way,
Morven stares with timeless gaze
Across the primeval landscape,
A giant of old
Who gives no secrets away.

When all is still
And hushed in sleep,
What memories of old
Linger in Morven's shade,
Far beyond the wayward city
Beyond the path of men.

Ronald Thomson.

A WEATHER EYE ON CAITHNESS

It's been a month for snatching the odd hour of sunshine between the squalls, always keeping a weather eye on the sky for sudden change.

A bright, very clear morning early in March gave us the incentive for a wander over Dorrery Hill even though it was snowing and blowing hard when we set off in the car. I'd been watching the skies closely though and for once my judgement was right that this was the last of the heavy showers, at least for an hour or two.

Although the smallest of hills, Dorrery can be a slog if you take the wrong route. It's best to set off from near the old Brawlbin School, crossing fields and aiming for the cairn on the skyline. Half a mile from the road is a monument to John Macdonald, Apostle of the North and Gaelic poet, who was born here a couple of hundred years ago. The grass-grown ruins of the village houses, just below steep heathery slopes, seem more like the remains of a prehistoric settlement than a home for people in such recent times.

There are little crags here; you could even kill yourself on them if you really tried. Above, a good cairn marks a much better top and viewpoint than the slightly higher summit, capped by mast and building, half a mile to the South.

The secret when carrying on to the mast is to first go down, then wend your way along below the crags, keeping off the crest of the ridge which gives very rough going. Later in the spring this is a particularly delightful route, with primroses and foxgloves on grassy rocky banks.

The view from Dorrery is out of all proportion to its height, especially on a clear blustery day with cumulonimbus shower clouds dramatising the landscape of yellows, browns and white mountains. You look out over all Caithness, across the flows and countless (well maybe 20) lochs over to Morven and Loyal and Hope to the Griams and Armine. Here is the boundary between the remote, empty country to the West and the farmland to the East.

The next shower was driving in fast, we sheltered from the hail and snow till the worst had passed then descended, past the heather slopes towards Brawlbin. There is a surprisingly large area of scrub willow here, lots of nooks and crannies, standing stones, mounds, an area that must once have been well known.

The shower cleared to that washed clear, bracing sunshine so characteristic of late winter/early spring. It's a rewarding time to make the effort to get out of doors.

A couple of weeks later I set off for Wick. It takes just 20 minutes in the car, an hour or so by bike. Yet in all my time in Caithness I'd never walked down the Wick river from Watten. Nor had I ever taken the train for the short journey from Wick to Georgemas. These people who never explore their own back yard!

The morning dawned cold, clear and frosty, with patchy, frozen snow. I set off first on a short round trip by car, leaving rucksack near the Bower quarry and a bike at Georgemas. This would allow me to run the first six miles over very familiar country, and provide me transport home from the station.

Unfortunately, my weather forecasting was less successful this time and, on arriving back home, it started to snow and blow hard. With rucksack and bike strategically placed, it was too late to back out, so somewhat grimly I set off jogging through the young blizzard which had suddenly replaced those exhilarating clear morning skies.

I was warm, but pretty wet by the time the snow-covered rucksack came into sight, an hour or so later. The sky was now starting to clear, and weather gradually improved as I made my way along the shore of Loch Watten at a more leisurely pace. The narrow strip of land between the railway and the loch provides a very pleasant walk, nobody goes there except fishermen.

The Wick River proved much better than expected and to walk its length gives a totally different impression of the country. Mostly the walking is good, there are stiles and bridges and only near Stirkoke were there some difficult, unbridged ditches to cross. In drier summer weather these would pose little problems.

The stretch between Watten and Bilbster is particularly good, the feel of some remote, upland strath as the river winds between heathery and grassy banks. A huge standing stone at Bilbster is worth detouring to look at. From here on, I kept north of the River, however it may be slightly easier to cross to the south bank by the footbridge near Ingimster.

Everywhere were birds, waders, ducks, geese in hundreds and whooper swans. Marshy pools near Stirkoke were particularly interesting. Beyond the railway bridge I scrambled up to the monument at Altimarlach, the site of the last clan battle in Scotland. A little further on, a good made path, with information boards, gives a pleasant last two miles down to Wick.

Black clouds had been gathering to the north and once again the hail and sleet swept down. Unprepared shoppers with bare heads hurried for shelter, I carried on, in tune with the river, not the town, out past the waterfront to finish the journey properly on the harbour breakwater, where the grey North Sea opened out from the river mouth.

It felt strange to get on the Sprinter – the 1535 hrs to Inverness for such a short journey, and even stranger to whisk the distance it had just taken me 6 hours to walk in 12 minutes. Who says the train is slow! It's much too fast to see anything but a glimpse of the country. Modern travel has done much to take away that sense of place. We can all do with making some regular journeys at good old-fashioned walking speed, at least once in a while.

Back at Georgemas, the hail was squalling down again, soon to turn to snow – just another dose of what's been a good, bracing month!

RALPH
(Reprinted from Caithness Courier).

THE GATEWAY TO CAITHNESS

Morven mounts guard and the wild seas enfold it and the winds blow fresh and clear over its lonely moors.

The lark sings and the sea-birds cry while the lowing of cattle and the bleating of sheep mingle with the sound of mower and tractor in their season.

Down from the hills through the Straths, tumble the peaty waters of the rivers, hurrying over their boulder-strewn beds, hastening towards the sea.

"Are there wild flowers in Caithness?" someone said to me. Of course there are. Primroses can be seen in profusion on the grassy banks of the streams. Primroses with wide bright eyes, gazing from among the moss and stones. Then the dog violet and the wild pansy, small but very lovely, raise their dainty heads by the wayside.

Take a walk up the Strath and in lonely isolated places there blooms the wild yellow iris.

The heather-spreading in purple splendour, with the bees busily extracting the honey from the minute bells. Also in their season come the bluebell and the harebell – blue as the summer sky. Even the purple poppy grows in thick clumps at the side of the farm road that leads up to the moorland. The buttercup and the daisy and the lovely marguerite growing among the varied colourful grasses. From all these Caithness flowers, there hangs on the air their lovely perfume; mingling with the scent of the clover, gorse, honeysuckle and the wild rose. Very sweetly the memory lingers and on cold and wintry days these wild flowers bring back the summer days with their glowing warmth and colour.

A.B. McLeod.

MAGIC OF CAITHNESS

NEIL GUNN (1891-1973)

You caught the Caithness image
    With a graceful pen
Pushed your ploughshare
    Through the cold earth
And rekindled the flame.

Under the open sky
    You sensed again
The salt sea-breeze
    Upon the face of youth
And knew its joy.

You saw your father
    Wrest from the living sea
The silver phosphorous harvest;
    Break bread after grace
For the bounty hard won.

The Dunbeath Strath -
    Where you roamed wild
Seeking the elusive salmon
    Casting your thoughts
Into the pool of life.

You saw the years ascend
    Like the morning sun
Yet sought to muse
    Upon the time-machine –
And you became a child again.

Ronald Thomson

CHAPTER 2
NEIL GUNN COUNTRY

In the summer of 1936, Neil Gunn made a return to grass roots – Dunbeath and its river. The result was a classic novel "Highland River" (1937) published in Edinburgh by the Porpoise Press.

The novel was not only an artistic and commercial success, but also gave Neil Gunn the impetus to become a full time writer.

Highland River is very much an evocation of Neil Gunn's childhood, set as it is in Dunbeath, although un-named in the novel.

In Herbert Sinclair's picture-book "Caithness Your Home" (1930), Neil contributed an interesting essay on the Dunbeath coast: he recalled the romance and danger of the sea, the excitement of seeing the fishing boats homeward bound (his father was a skipper) and the harvest which enriched the community.

Into that self same sea "clear and deep and drowning" came the river which fascinated Neil Gunn. It may be remembered that Gunn's first Caithness novel appeared in 1926 under the title of "The Grey Coast" and in 1931 the more notable "Morning Tide". The latter may be regarded as a stepping stone toward "Highland River" although each novel is distinct in its own right.

In August 1987, I took a hike up the Dunbeath Strath to get an idea of the locale which inspired Neil Gunn. After a light lunch at the Dunbeath Hotel, I wandered down by the old stone bridge which is on the A9 route to Wick.

Dunbeath is one of those places on the Caithness map which are rooted in the herring days. Wick, of course, was the premier centre for the "boom century" as it has been called – but coastal villages like Dunbeath, Latheronwheel, and even more notably Lybster, had a part to play.

Neil has written in "Highland River" – "strength was the keynote of this coast, a passionless remorseless strength, unyielding as the rock" and those graphic words convey a true picture of the Far North.

Though Neil Gunn only lived in Caithness until he was about 12 years of age, he never forgot the Dunbeath of his childhood: its people, coastline, river and strath, were vital impressions which influenced his literary work.

Neil Miller Gunn was born on November 8th, 1891. He was one of nine children to James and Isabella Gunn. In 1904, Neil went to live with his married sister, Mary, and her husband in Galloway. Years later, he began his career with the Customs and Excise Service and settled in the Highlands.

Short story writing attracted Neil Gunn's pen and his work appeared in such magazines as the Cornhill Magazine, Northern Review and the Scots Magazine.

His Caithness novels, however, established his name to the public at large and remain among his best work.

My first visit to the Strath was in June 1987, with my twin brother Alan, but due to uncertain weather we didn't venture as far as I would have liked.

However, the scene had a more promising look second time round, and a glimpse of the sun seemed like a good omen.

On the earlier visit, the river was low near Dunbeath, but in August it flowed more invitingly by the over-hanging trees and narrow path.

Dark water, white flecked, ran between stones of varying size, while here and there some yellow "weeds" struck a welcome note.

Further upstream, the river tumbled down a miniature staircase, while at the same time a tributary sent a constant flow of rushing water into the Highland River Neil Gunn knew so well.

After the first footbridge is crossed, the Strath changes character, there is a profusion of bracken and trees along the route, and one noticed a stray rabbit dart into the undergrowth.

It was a little world on its own, a Caithness wilderness which seemed half-forgotten, shadowed by antique trees – and yet its own timeless companion was the river of life.

A second bridge affords a fine view of the river winding its way downstream. The current is robust and the sound a pervading one along the route.

Part of the walk led through a plethora of trees which overshadowed the view ahead, as the winding path skirted the river below.

Speaking of trees, Dunbeath is listed as the "Hill of birches" in that fine reference book "The County of Caithness" (1907) which was edited by the late John Horne. Certainly the Strath has more trees than you will see along many a Caithness mile.

After the avenue of trees, the scene opens to a good sweep of the river, and on a hillside a large house overlooks the vista. The mansion house intrigued me, it was notable along the walk. Who owns it, or how long it has been there, remains a question, but its vantage point on the

Dunbeath River is indeed memorable.

Perhaps the house may be the shooting lodge referred to in "Highland River" where the boys could never rid themselves of the impression of "its windows as eyes".

The afternoon lived up to its promise and I discarded my jacket in the warm air. Once over the brae I took a "breather" and surveyed the scene: below me was a rusty iron bridge which skirted the river, and nearby a sheep and her lamb grazed, then aware of my presence, departed.

The Strath gave way to steep hillsides, and another phase of the route appeared in prospect; but I decided on a round trip of two hours – and it was time to return to Dunbeath.

A last photographic souvenir seemed in order, and I crossed a small bridge, which was in an unsafe condition toward the opposite bank.

The river was placid facing downstream, although a tributary joined it from the hillside. A "pool" of ink-black water, laced with white, framed by stone-work and trees, suggested an interesting composition for the camera.

Neil Gunn knew the terrain (and further up the Strath) like the back of his hand. His novel is rich in detail where the central figure – "Kenn" – discovers the river as a source of adventure "often intense and always secretive".

The intermix between Kenn's boyhood and manhood is skilfully achieved by Gunn in an unusual and original novel which gained him the James Tait Black Memorial Prize.

Dedicated to his brother John, "Highland River" offers the reader Neil Gunn's most intimate view of Dunbeath, its river and strath.

A few years after the publication of "Highland River" came Neil Gunn's epic novel, also set in Caithness, "The Silver Darlings" (1941) a tale of the herring fishers, notably dedicated to his father who was a Dunbeath skipper.

"Morning Tide", "Highland River" and "The Silver Darlings" each in their way contribute to a picture of Neil Gunn's native land, that haunt of dashing seas, distant horizons, and Highland River, "far from the madding crowd".

R.T.

The coast between Lybster and Wick meanders through countryside bordered by the open sea. It is crofting country, very much an echo of old Caithness. Strange to think there used to be a railway line along the route – but there was indeed and it was famous in its day – the Lybster Line!

"Tempus fugit" was not its motto, probably "all in good time" might be nearer the mark. It was however a welcome link for eastcoasters: its main purpose was the fish trade, but it serviced passengers too.

The Wick and Lybster Light Railway, to give it its official name, was 13¾ miles long and built at a cost of £70,000. This rural service began on 3rd July 1903, and continued until 1st April, 1944. Caithness writer, John Horne described it as a "glorious institution" – for the relaxed passage of the train pleased him very much.

Someone with vivid memories of the Lybster Line is Caithness exile S. Miller Gault:

"You can still see where the single track ran as you go along the A9 near Occumster, there is the space where it used to be near Ulbster school, as you go north it nearly comes on to the road and runs alongside as you approach Thrumster. I can see it as I write, the little tank engine, steam of course, the two, three, or four small carriages, no corridor, of course, a convenience would be inconvenient on such a short line. Lybster, Occumster, Mid-Clyth, Ulbster, Thrumster and the old grey town of Wick, it was part of the life of the good people who lived and worked on the crofts. Few carried watches, except on the Sabbath day when the men had a waistcoat on, so they knew the time near enough by the train. The crofter who had recently acquired a horse, generally of mixed blood a cross between a Garron pony and a Clydesdale, used to take it up to the nearest road to the railway line and await a passing train to see if it would take fright. If the animal stood firm it would be kept, rated as reliable, and not returned to the seller.

When I went to school in Wick we travelled on the Lybster Line. John Skene was the engine driver and John Mackay was guard and everybody's friend. You could see him coming up the platform in Wick his arms overflowing with parcels, anything not available in the local shops in Lybster was obtained thus.

On odd occasions as a special favour, I travelled home in the Guard's Van and in repayment, had to throw out newspapers at intervals on the line where they were picked up by the awaiting recipients. How we boys used to admire John's prowess when, after waving his green flag, he could board the speeding train without any bother.

On market day in Wick, picking up the stirks in a cattle truck was quite an adventure. Hanging on the truck was John, waving his arm frantically to the engine driver to get up speed to send the truck from the siding on to the line by means of a rope which he slipped off at the crucial moment and braked the truck in time not to send the guard's van spinning back down the line. It always looked dangerous. I think we expected an accident to happen sometime but it never did.

John Mackay, Guard on the Lybster Line for many years, everybody's friend, sleeps with many of them peacefully in the quiet little cemetery in Mid Clyth. The Lybster Line has gone perhaps for ever, but the memory remains."

Lybster was at one time second only to Wick as a fishing centre. In historian Calder's day the village had a population of some 800 people, and the number of fishing boats in the season was upwards of 200. The "herring days" really put Lybster on the map; previous to that, the district had been of little note. The success of inshore herring fishing changed the whole picture, and by 1817, the Fishery Board for Scotland recognised Lybster as a Fishing Station. Within Lybster's jurisdiction, came Clyth, Forse, Swiney and Latheronwheel. By 1833 Lybster was the third best fished Station in Scotland – surpassed by Wick and Fraserburgh.

It was not only the fishermen who benefitted, but the community at large, and the New Statistical Account of Scotland (1840) reveals some interesting data on the subjects. In 1838, there was 76 fishing boats at Dunbeath, 35 at Latheronwheel, 32 at Forse, 10 at Swiney, 101 at Lybster, 53 at Clyth, and 18 at East Clyth, in all a total of 325 boats. There was 1,321 fishermen, 106 coopers, 937 women as packers, and 178 labourers, in all 2,540 persons – plus about 50 fish curers. The number of barrels cured at the above was 39,093.

In those palmy days of the herring season, men from Lewis and Harris came to the east coast of Caithness – and Lybster had its share of them. They were like the local fishermen, deeply religious in character:

Even at sea it was not unusual for them to engage in the singing of psalms followed by prayer after they had shot the nets.

Those days were Lybster's notable time, and anyone who wishes to trace the Caithness heritage might include a visit to Lybster – quiet though it be today.

Speaking of the Latheron district brings to mind a Caithness worthy, the late Willie Sinclair, who hailed from that part of the county. I only knew Willie in the autumn of his days but was impressed by his personality. We exchanged letters and met a few times at his Bonar Bridge, Sutherland home, where he lived with his wife, Jean.

This ex-soldier (a veteran of two world wars) and keen gardener, had a fund of stories about the old days . . . be it home or abroad. He lived in Canada between the Wars and recalled a trip home in 1932, when the train had an hour's stop at Jasper in the Rockies. Willie, garbed in the kilt, wandered along the platform to admire the scenery . . .

"I noticed a fine burly figure in police uniform approaching, and in doing cut in to rub shoulders with me, and addressed me thus: "Yer goan Home" – pure Caithness in the midst of a welter of tongues, mostly from the USA. I replied "yes" at the same time trying to recall whom I had before me.

At last the Truant Memory came to my aid. Aye! It was Dan Henderson, a noted cyclist around the games in the post-war years. We had a rare crack."

Willie remembered Vancouver as a Caithness haven where "each and every home made us welcome. There he recalled those days and ways, the colourful characters, the songs, the stories, all those rich ingredients which made Caithness so distinctive and precious."

Willie once penned some "Causeymire Memories" which included an anecdote told to him by Alex Sutherland of Rhianacoil. It was about 1906, the year Bostock and Wombell's Circus visited Caithness, and the day was a Sunday when they left Thurso via the Causeymire. At the "Meeting House", a church service was underway when someone spotted the cavalcade led by an old elephant. The service was suspended while the congregation and minister went outside for a view of this unusual occurence. A "red letter day" for the Rangag community.

MEMORY PICTURES

Mist shrouded mountains
　　Heather-clad braes,
Ruined crofts, long deserted
　　Where sheep quietly graze.

Sun-dappled moorlands,
　　Cloud-clustered skies,
Empty straths, silence shattered
　　By gulls plaintive cries.

Bright berried rowans,
　　Foxgloves in ranks,
Noisy burns rushing
　　Twixt primrose-starred banks.

Winter winds keening,
　　Frost-sparkled earth;
Summer breezes playing
　　O'er moon-silvered Firth.

Cliff-sheltered harbours,
　　Boats at the quay,
Lone beaches, forgotten,
　　Caressed by the sea.

Softly, unbidden,
　　The heart to possess,
Come memory pictures
　　Of haunting Caithness.

Maureen Nugent.

HORIZONS

"The flatness of the county opens up some wonderful horizons. From scores of view-points the sun may be seen rising – out of the sea, from the broad moorland, over wandering hills, or across unmolested fields. All along the east coast especially, the seascape is almost beyond praise. A summer sunrise seen from some eastern ledge, or from the hills behind, is a life-time's rapture."

How well John Horne reflected the beauty – and the magic of

Caithness. An abiding memory was a sunrise over Wick Bay: "All the sea-floor radiates in the glory, and the sky-colours melt into whiteness; over land and sea, rock and cloud, above and around, it is day."

To fully savour the seascapes of the North one should view them in the dawn or sunset, when sea and sky are one. Few of us make the effort to witness the dawn of a new day, to rise early and enjoy what the poet, James Thomson[1], (1700-45) described as "the cool, the fragrant, and the silent hour" – but well we might.

The American philosopher, H. D. Thoreau, considered the dawn his favourite time, or season, of the day. It awoke in him a spirit of renewal.

Those who feel a flat landscape has little or nothing to offer – should look and think again. Certainly Caithness has a beauty of her own, a beauty distinctive and notable, impressive under the northern light.

Good weather is a variable thing in Caithness, thus a fine day is something to be cherished, for when the sun shines it seems like a benediction on this land of distant horizons.

It was good to relax in the cool air-conditioned comfort of my uncle's drawing room, after the humid heat of Chicago.

We had arrived back the 85 miles out of the city after a day's shopping and sightseeing, finishing with a sumptuous dinner in his very exclusive club. The expensive perfume of the elegantly groomed and bejewelled ladies and the luxuriously appointed and highly scented powder rooms still clung to my nostrils. As we merged on to the street, with its myraid lanes of roaring traffic, the hot air hit me like a blast from a furnace and I cricked by neck backwards as far as I could searching for a vestige of sky between the towering skyscrapers and a breath of fresh air to soothe my jaded lungs.

We were to have an evening's viewing, with invited friends, of my uncle's collection of film slides – one of undoubted interest, for he had travelled all over the world. We looked forward to viewing the great sights of Berlin, Paris, Madrid, Rio and the Grand Canyon – all were due to appear on the programme with my uncle as commentator.

Imagine my surprise and emotion as the first picture to flash upon the screen was the cool green and white of our Caithness croft – its white-washed walls and maroon-painted door basking tranquilly in its neat walled garden, with its rows of vegetables bordered by beds of marigolds, michaelmas daisies and sweet mignonette. There was our fragrant honeysuckle peeping at the livingroom window and my mother's favourite red tea rose climbing over the sill of the bedroom

---

[1]*James Thomson: "The Seasons".*

window. Blackcurrant and gooseberry bushes rambled in wild profusion along the garden walls.

Beyond the garden, the green fields, dotted with white sheep grazing peacefully like a great flower-patterned quilt, fell away to the blue line of the sea - the broad vista of the Moray Firth stretching from Noss Head in the north east to Tarbat Ness in the south. What tales of triumph and tragedy lay concealed by those deceptively limpid waters! To the north, on the far horizons at Hillhead was that a faint trail of smoke – like an Indian smoke signal – heralding the arrival of the Lybster train – the old Coffee Pot as she was affectionately dubbed. Even at this distance my ears strained automatically for the sound of its heavy-puffing and its shrill whistle as it climbed the gradient coming into view at the top of Hillhead before running down into Lybster station. In those days, far better than our clocks – which never worked – its twice daily journeys between Wick and Lybster set the time and pattern of our day and our trips on this black, fire-breathing monster became the principal excitement and gateway to the great events in our lives.

Through our garden gate, my eye wandered down the familiar pathway to the green rolling braes below our house, sheep spangled and dotted with primroses and in summer would explode into a riot of colour – with a profusion of sea pinks, campion, saxifrage, cornflowers, heartease, wild violets – down to the little beach with an iron bollard driven into the rocks, once used as a landing stage for our fishing boats. I could still feel the smell of the tangle and the warmth of the sun-backed rocks as we basked in our summer sun, singing to an inquisitive seal popping its head out of the water. We could climb the giant staircase cut into the rock where it had been excavated to provide material for the building of Lybster harbour over a century before – some said, more romantically than truthfully, perhaps, to pave the great streets of London. What a strain it must have been for the horses pulling these rock-laden carts up these steep braes for it would have been too slow and impractical a process to have transported the rock by sea.

Back along the cliff-top – a favourite walk of our almost tame otter – to the top of the brae down which we would roll to the harbour, nestling cosily between its two sheltering cliffs – a one time hive of industry, alive with fishing boats, fishermen, fish and screeching seagulls and the smell and smoke of the now long defunct kippering kiln.

To school, up the Shore Road, we would pass over the Reisgill Burn, a magnificent, thundering waterfall when in full spate and a dangerous challenge to venturesome explorers. Its steep banks, smothered in primroses in spring, became a magnificent wild garden in summer, covered with rowans and wild hazelnuts in autumn and its pools frozen over in winter, an explorers paradise for all seasons. Viewed from the water's edge below, the General Wade bridge which spanned it towered like a Chicago skyscraper above us. Who could resist the death-defying challenge of running along its narrow parapet when one false slip meant certain death? Or the forays along the burn itself, up the waterfall or even the icy chill of its treacherous brown pools if one fell in? Bless those forbearing, if grumbling, teachers who dried us out round the classroom stove to save us from a worse fate on arrival home!

Home – back to that white-washed cottage, its fresh green fields and its peaceful sheep portrayed on the wide cine-screen. The strains of J.S. Bach's "Sheep may safely graze" kept running through my head as I glanced at my uncle, pointer in hand ready to begin his commentary. Was there the glint of a tear in his eye, or a tremor in the voice of this hardened, self-made American as he began with the opening words "This is my ancestral home".

Janet Mackay
The above article was awarded 2nd prize in the Alan Thomson Memorial Competition (Published in John O'Groat Journal), 1989

Caithness has been dubbed "the land of 100 lochs" – an intriguing title indeed. The county is well known for its trout fishing (the season lasts from March till October) and two angling centres are Watten and Halkirk.

For those interested in salmon fishing, Thurso river may well be the venue and who knows with what return – the Queen Mother has fished many times on this river which is the longest in Caithness.

It's interesting to note that some of the best sea-angling is in the Pentland Firth and the sea off Duncansby Head is the deepest anywhere along the east coast of Britain[1].

But let us return to those 100 lochs we began with – which is the largest of them? That honour belongs to Watten, which is almost three miles long and famous for its brown trout. Watten village is a quiet retreat at the south east end of the loch, and some 7 miles WNW of Wick.

To see trout fishers on Loch Watten is a timeless picture indeed. The fishermen in their small boats, on the spacious loch, might be a picture from some mythical land where there is no north or south, east or west, for in a poetic sense – is not a loch a little world of its own?

And to watch a sunset at Loch Watten, is an experience not to be missed by the novice visitor or seasoned holiday-maker to Caithness.

[1]*"From Five to Sixty Fathoms Deep" – Caithness Explorer Magazine.*

"Clyth – the forgotten harbour way down the cliffs". *Photographed by Dan Mackay.*

Impressive is the cliff scenery at Whaligoe , and the 300 odd flagstone steps which lead down the cliffside. From the foot of the stairway to the sea, you step onto a small precinct where fishing nets were dried, and boats laid up, but that is all in the past. The restless sea looks especially grand and presents a vivid picture of nature at work. That view alone makes a visit to Whaligoe well worthwhile.

Whaligoe was another link in the east coast fishing days of the 19th century. Hardy indeed must have been the fisherwomen who climbed the cliff steps with a creel on their backs and maybe a gale in progress!

You won't find Whaligoe steps sign-posted but for those interested they may be found $6\frac{1}{2}$ miles south of Wick (A9 route) at Ulbster. Fine to visit this former fishing creek on a good day, but in winter the sea spray rises over the cliff top, and those are high cliffs at Whaligoe!

Those who wish to visit the Whaligoe steps should bear in mind they are bereft of handrail, and are no place for the very young or infirm, but with care can be recommended. It's also worth taking a camera to record this unusual part of Caithness, where the zig-zag formation of steps descend to the northern sea: a stairway steeped in the past.

The imprint of old Caithness seems most poignant in a ruined croft – dwellings which were home for an earlier generation – now long deserted and open to the sky.

From humble homes as these came forth God-fearing people drawing their living from the land and sea, as their fathers had done before them; their pleasures were simple, their contentment based on honest toil, with the hope of good days for their children who worked south or emigrated to the New World.

Around many a peat fire Caithness yarns would be exchanged and dwelt upon, a friend or stranger made welcome.

It was a caring community with hospitality at its core – neighbour helped neighbour – and there was a richness of spirit among the people.

Sentiment may heighten the picture now, but in those unvarnished days the crofting and fishing people left a worthy reputation for character and integrity in a changing world.

And from the croftlands, who could forget those magical days of summer and memorable seascapes luring the eye to distant horizons, or perhaps at sunset an armada of brown sailed boats* in quest of the "silver darlings" – that staple meal of countless Caithnessians – the herring!

CAITHNESS SEA

Bold is the Caithness Sea
Which beats upon the shore,
And flings its spray
Upon the rocks of old,
With unyielding passion –
Strong and vibrant as youth.

Bold is the Caithness sea
Which sweeps across the sand,
Each wave that rises forth
Laced with green and gold,
All with dash and vigour
At the North winds command!

Bold is the Caithness sea
Alive with a zest for life,
By rock, cliff, or goe,
Fresh as the caller wind.
Timeless this potent force
Transcends the will of man.

Ronald Thomson.

Strength was the keynote of this coast, a passionless remorseless strength, unyielding as the rock, tireless as the water; the unheeding rock that a falling body would smash itself to pulp upon; the transparent water that would suffocate an exhausted body in the slow rhythm of its swirl. There was a purity about it all, stainless as the gull's plumage, wild and cold as its eye. However strange and haunted one's thoughts, they were never really introverted; but, rather, lifted into some new dimensions of the purely objective, where internal heats and involutions pass out upon, without tainting, the wind and the sea.

This cool rarefied poising of life upon death had its summer days of exquisite beauty. These days were never sought for deliberately; they came by chance or inspiration. An urge to bathe, then to follow sheep tracks, to go on . . . and presently a cliff-top cradled the body under a sun whose heat was tempered by the sea's breath. There to lie extended above the uprising floor of the ocean was to experience the lovely sensation of floating between earth and heaven, as lonely gulls high overhead breasted the sun in snow-white arcs. Even the crying of the gulls down in the rocks grew faint with sunny distance, became the echo of an echo of something forever lost. Yet not entirely lost, as if the forlorn wave of the cry had buoyancy in it and bore the body to far shores of sleep. And the body gave way to this with worldless bliss, yet upon that bliss nothing carnal intruded. No hot vision came stirring young flesh to secret images. How could it, out of that near green and remote blue sea, out of echoing caverns, out of tides that swung to the changing phases of the moon?

There is strangeness and mystery here; it is overwrought with human emotion. It is directed inward and down, not outward to sea and sky. It does not race in wheels of light on the waters or pass away on the wind like a murmur. Its rhythm is the human cry against the dark imprisoning rock; not the freedom that passes into the sunlight, into the loveliness that is untainted as the sea, heedless of life or death, cool, passionless, remaining, and passing on.

Neil M. Gunn (Highland River).

MAGIC OF CAITHNESS

Sarclet Loch near Thrumster is the venue for model yacht racing in Caithness, and the scene is inviting as brightly coloured yachts enliven this quiet corner of Caithness. Artistically, the subject is ideal on a fine summer day, and one could imagine it as inspiration for the French impressionists, certainly the mood, colour and movement has an attraction of its own.

In 1982, a meeting at Sarclet was cancelled – due to the lack of wind! Seldom in Caithness does that occur, anyway, this prompted thoughts back to that northern loch, and its yachts, and our holiday excursion there, and the end result was a little poem in tribute:

MODEL YACHTS AT SARCLET

Yachts traverse the azure loch
    Sleek and sure and trim,
Yachts which might remind Gulliver
    Of some miniature armada,
Seem to me impressive
    Under the summer sun.

Fair is the race
    That lifts the heart again,
The joy of man and boy
    Spirit of the game;
Swift-winged the boats
    Write poetry of their own.

In the mosaic of Caithness
    May there always be,
Those little bright yachts
    Windblown across the loch,
Little yachts of Sarclet
    Which gladden the inward eye.

Ronald Thomson.

CHAPTER 3
DAYS LANG SYNE

The Edinburgh Caithness magazines are a valuable source of rich nostalgia for anyone interested in the county, and the 1952 issue features an article entitled: "Those were the Days or were They?" which will remind one generation and enlighten another.

"It was one afternoon just past the middle of November, I put my head close to an open window in a corridor of the train which was dragging its way to Georgemas. You know how the train "drags" once you pass Forsinard. Three breathfuls of that air I inhaled, the air full of that which I had missed for a fortnight or more in London – a fresh coolness, impregnated with something from the brown heather. Then I shut the window, went into the compartment, and sat down in a corner with my legs resting on the opposite seat. Yes this was Caithness; but was it my Caithness?

The Caithness when I was a boy, when there were no "buses to take you to school, when you never had the opportunity of turning up your nose at good food at a feeding centre, when in the wintertime you maybe had tatties and herring three times a week, broth and beef on a Sunday, (with the broth heated up on the Monday), with hard cod and tatties.

Periodically, cabbage and ham-end with plenty of oatbread, plenty of porridge (made as porridge should be made, not this modern five-minute substitute), sooans and broonplate, croppan-head and fish soup, haddies rolled in four and grilled on a brander, clap-shot as I knew it – mashed tatties and swedes, with butter, pepper and salt, and very often mixed with some Armour's tinned roast-beef, something far better than the later corned beef, oat bannocks with a liberal coating of butter, croodie and sugar and all the rest of the fare that set us out in the world, fit physically and mentally."

From food my memory went to the games we played, happy pastimes of the long ago which find no place in the childhood of the Caithness of today. Our games were seasonal. There was the time when kites were flown, handmade kites, with the head made from the wooden hoop of a herring barrel, with a paper covering most likely of the "Northern Ensign", and a long string of tails from that same newspaper.

The time when you took out your iron hoop, made by John Macdonald ("Zulu") or other blacksmith, which you guided along with a cleek or a bit of wood or metal. You walked on stilts, made often from a couple of unplanned staves which went to make up a herring barrel. "Knotty" you enjoyed, a rough kind of shinty. There was the season for marbles, and you had the millionaire feeling when your aim was unerring and you had won many marbles from your boy friends.

Rounders we played, and the hide-and-seek games of "geg smuggle" and "high-spy" or maybe it was "I-spy". We caught "brannals" up the Riverside, and sillocks at one or other of the small harbours which adorned the north side of Wick Bay. We "laid" nets with the fishermen on a Saturday afternoon, and on a Monday morning, helped to "lift" the nets, with maybe a "sail" on the top of the nets to the Harbour.

We bought a pennyworth of "chipped aipples" or broken biscuits from Willie Nicolson or Sinclair Brothers. The pie shops of Mrs Dallas and Jinny Oal were but a hazy memory to us, but there were Betsy Mowat's tippeny muttoners and a bottle of lemonade – when somebody made us rich with a sixpence.

We had the Band of Hope soirees, the magic lantern entertainments

Wick Bridge Street, *drawing by Jack Sinclair.*

in the Temperance Hall, the Fergusmas Market and the Hill Market, the old Market Place filled with shows and tents during the fishing season and joy in our hearts and nothing in our pockets . . . in days when Caithness was my Caithness."

W.P.B.

I owe a great deal in spirit to the Edinburgh Caithness Magazines, and notably to Mother's writings, prose and poetry which appeared there. Alan and myself were also contributors.

Sadly, the magazine ceased from November 1995 – it had appeared for Caithness Exiles since the 1950 issue. A remarkable achievement.

R.T.

Wick Bridge Street – modern view.
Photographed by Ronald Thomson.

Old Parish Church Wick (1830).

THE SEAGULL

I fly before the mast
  My wings
Dip to the salt storm
  Wildness and winter, my delight
Exchange for spring
  Their curded, scudding drifts
Of spumy spray.

I float in pools of sun
  Dyed in hyacinth blue:
Summer – content
My wings close-furled in quiet,
  Shut to the rocking cadence my bright eye.

Heaven holds from me the gift
  Of man's warm tears.
My song shrieks hard on the gale:
  I know the unriven rock
Yet, when my young ones call
  I turn, I am.

Arthur Ball.
(Reprinted from Scots Magazine)

If there is one sound which reflects the character of Wick, it is the seagull with its haunting cry, for Wick is a fishing town at heart. True, its glory as a herring port – the great "Herringopolis" of Scotland – has long since gone, but its heritage lives on regardless.

Wick has been a Royal Burgh since 1589, by decree of King James VI of Scotland; the original "town" lay north of Wick river, and according to historian Calder, probably had the appearance of a "mean-looking village". The town's position held the key to its future prosperity: for along its rugged coast, a rich harvest would be gleaned – of herring – otherwise known as "The Silver Darlings"!

The name Wick was well chosen: it derives from The Scandinavian "Vik" which means an opening or bay, another reminder of the county's Norse heritage.

Strictly speaking, the herring trade did not begin at Wick proper, but nearby Staxigoe, a fishing village two miles north-east of Wick. As Calder points out there was no harbour at Wick "except the mouth of the river" thus Staxigoe became the first fishing station in Caithness, and at one time letters for Wick were addressed "By Staxigoe".

Though the herring industry did not reach its zenith until the 19th century, its history may be traced back to 1767, when Alexander Miller of Staxigoe, John Sutherland of Wester and John Anderson of Wick, began fishing with two small sloops on the north coast. Thus began for the people of the Far North, the most notable chapter in her history.

Wick – County Town of Caithness lies 21 miles south of John O'Groats – different in character to its sister town, Thurso, it has notable appeal in its coastal situation, and also Riverside – place of County Shows, and former gala days.

The Riverside is especially memorable on a fine summer evening. A stroll along by the Calder statue overlooking Wick Old Parish Church, and thence by the Coghill Bridge – with its grand vista upstream – is well worthwhile for the visitor, and rewarding indeed for the Caithness exile.

R.L.S. IN PULTENEYTOWN

It was R.L. Stevenson who dubbed Wick "one of the meanest of man's towns . . . on the baldest of God's bays" – it was a retrospective view written many years after his six-week stay in the autumn of 1868.

Why he came to Scotland's herring capital as an 17-year-old youth, and how it impressed him, is something of a story in itself, and one which has intrigued me for many years.

It was during Stevenson's vacation from Edinburgh University that he visited the Wick breakwater then under construction by his father's firm, Thomas Stevenson & Co., Leith.

RLS had no desire to become a civil engineer, but to please his father, he had visited the breakwater at Anstruther, and now came his venture to Caithness.

It is likely Stevenson and his father sailed from Leith – this was the quickest and most direct route – bearing in mind there was no railway to Wick until 1874.

Stevenson has recorded in "Random Memories" that Caithness in his time was visited by only the sportsman or antiquarian. Yet Wick did have its influx of outsiders during the herring season: from Orkney and Shetland, the Western Isles and from Moray and Banff.

Statistics are impressive – herring caught during the season ranged from 100,000 to 120,000 barrels and people partially or wholly employed, totalled around 12,000. This Boom Century, as it has been called, reached its zenith in 1862, when over 1000 boats sailed from Pulteneytown.

I say Pulteneytown, rather than Wick, for although one town physically, they were administered as separate burghs and did not

Photo of Robert Louis Stevenson (1850-1894).

amalgamate until 1902.

Pulteneytown, designed by the great Thomas Telford, and named after Sir William Pulteney who was chairman of the British Fisheries Society, was divided into Upper Pulteney and Lower – the latter being the harbour area where RLS resided.

The house where Stevenson lived is now occupied by the Customs and Excise. In 1868 it was a Temperance Hotel on Shore Road (now Harbour Terrace) where RLS enjoyed a superb view from the upper right hand window of his room.

Although the flat land of Caithness had no appeal for him, he did find interest in the rugged cliff scenery and vibrant sea vistas and reckoned that hanging around harbour-sides was "the richest form of idling".

On three successive afternoons RLS walked to Noss Head, where he saw the ruins of Castles Sinclair and Girnigoe. Just below there he discovered a refuge from the persistent wind and he writes engagingly of the contrast: "There, in the bleak and gusty north, I received, perhaps, my strongest impression of peace. I saw the sea to be great and calm; and the earth, in that little corner, was all alive and friendly to me."

The above quotation comes from Stevenson's 1874 essay "On the Enjoyment of Unpleasant Places"; 14 years passed before his second Caithness memoir, "Random Memories – The Education of an Engineer" appeared.

By the time Stevenson was writing his first letter home, on Friday, 28th August, his father had left for Edinburgh. Among those who befriended RLS were Sheriff Russel and his wife (friends of his father), and supervising engineer, Mr Macdonald – and it was their sons who were Stevenson's companions.

In another letter he writes of two very tiring days at the breakwater, one which was like mid-winter, with incessant rain, working from 10 a.m. to 2 p.m. and 3 p.m. to 7 p.m. out in the lighter or small boat, in a heavy sea. The physical effort left him unable to write home and he almost fell asleep after dinner. His hands were "skinned, blistered, discoloured and engrained with tar". Yet he took all this in good part, despite the weather and work involved.

What did RLS look like as an 17-year-old? Reports indicate that he was a slim, delicate-looking youth, with longish fair hair (this darkened in time) and that he wore a velvet coat.

Perhaps the most unforgettable character he met during his Pulteneytown days was the matriarch of the tinker families – Peggy Soo – who regaled RLS with a fund of Caithness tales. She remembered Stevenson as "a fine gentleman" who gave her sixpences for whisky!

RLS refers to the tinkers' cavern (on the South Head of Wick Bay) in

"Random Memories" and noted that you might see the women tending their fire and the men sleeping off their "coarse potations" – it must have been a rough existence for the tinker clan who made it their home for more than a century.

More than 30 years after Stevenson's visit, Peggy Soo – real name Margaret Newlands – was still pottering about Wick. Her age was thought to be close on 100.

Stevenson's letters from Pulteneytown, to his mother, have a vivid quality. Take, for example, this extract:

"I stood a long while on the cope, watching the sea below me; I hear its dull, monotonous roar at this moment below the shrieking of the wind; and there came ever recurring to my mind the verse I am so fond of:

> But yet the Lord that is on high
> Is more of might by far
> Than noise of many waters is
> Or great sea-billows are.

"The thunder at the wall when it first struck – the rush along ever growing higher – the great jet of snow white spray some 40 feet above you – and the "noise of many waters", the roar, the hiss, the "shrieking" among the shingle as it fell head over the heels at your feet."

RLS was in Caithness all September and early October. The weather appears to have been poor to harsh much of the time. He did in fact dub Wick a "sub-arctic town", but admitted that the lively winds made another boy of him.

1868 was really a coming of age for RLS – first at Anstruther, then at Pulteneytown. He was away from home, friends and familiar places; but the deeper imprint was made in Caithness – a world away from Heriot Row and the capital's Victorian middle class society.

Unforgettable was Stevenson's undersea debut in Wick Bay. Donning diver's suit and helmet (the latter almost floored him) RLS in company with one Bob Bain descended the ladder into a dream, fantasy experience, where sign language was the password.

Despite 20lbs. on each foot, a formidable helmet, not forgetting breast and back weights, Stevenson was amazed to discover how buoyant a diver could be and he recounts this experience superbly in "Random Memories".

His analogy about trying, and failing, to catch the elusive fish which darted before him – "swift as humming birds" – proves once again his apt, picturesque style of writing.

Few might have guessed in that autumn of 1868 that the Wick breakwater would never reach completion – for great seastorms tore it asunder – and eventually, after years of work and great expense, the project was abandoned.

Yet what is one failure, measured against a lifetime's achievement? In lighthouse building, the name of Stevenson remains of the highest calibre. The lighthouses at Holborn Head, Scrabster and Dunnet Head are reminders of their work in Caithness.

RLS seems to have made the most of his time in Caithness, be it watching an open-air Gaelic service in Wick; or taking a stagecoach to Thurso via Castletown village, where sand was blowing through the streets; or seeing a schooner ashore at Shaltigoe – nor forgetting his outdoor work at the breakwater in inclement weather. This and much more made his Caithness interlude a voyage of discovery and something which inspired some of his best writing.

RLS admitted that "six weeks in one unpleasant countryside had done more, it seemed, to quicken and educate my sensibilities than many years in places that jumped more nearly with my inclination".

Pulteneytown is a shadow of the past today, but the Caithness writings of Robert Louis Stevenson remain as vivid and memorable as the day they were written.

Reprinted from the Scots Magazine (1994). R.T.
Stevenson's Caithness Letters: See volume one of the Letters of Robert Louis Stevenson, edited by Bradford A. Booth and Ernest Mehew, published by Yale University Press in 1994.

JAMES BREMNER

Perhaps the most remarkable resident of Pulteneytown was James Bremner (1784-1856), harbour-builder and shipwreck raiser. His memorial credits Bremner with saving many lives, and refloating 256 stranded or sunken vessels, including the largest ship of his day "The Great Britain".

An interesting article in the Glasgow Caithness Magazine (Div Ye Mind?) by John Mowat, recalls how the "Great Britain" foundered on the Irish Coast in 1846, and remained there for almost a year until the ship-owners turned to "the wizard in the Far North" – James Bremner.

Within three months Bremner succeeded where others had failed, and the five-masted iron leviathan, 600 feet long ship was towed off by two Navy ships to Liverpool.

Bremner Salvage equipment seemed uncouth to the experts, but he had an instinctive genius and practical know-how, which held him in good stead. Bremner patented a number of inventions related to harbour work and contributed models to the Great Exhibition of 1851.

A man of Christian belief, he extended help to many: his harbour place home was often a refuge for shipwrecked mariners and the socially deprived.

Well may he be remembered.

WICK PRE 1914

There are those who can look back on the halcyon days of Wick and present a vivid picture which speaks for itself: take for example this memoir of Wick at the turn of the century. "Our youth was bounded by the sea. The Bay lay in front of us and there was the boundless North Sea to the horizon and beyond. From our vantage point on the north braes, in the long, halcyon, summer days, we watched the many types of vessels which came from north and south to enter the harbour or to anchor in the bay.

In addition to the countless fishing craft, under sail and in steam, local and stranger, which entered the harbour daily, there were cargo boats, laden with coal from the Tyne, salt from Runcorn and staves from Stavanger. Fishery Cruisers and Lighthouse vessels Norma and Hesperus would anchor in the Bay for a brief spell, as would also Grimsby trawlers (GY) and Aberdeen liners (A) on their way to the farther north fishing grounds. At unexpected intervals, the slate coloured Channel Fleet in all their might of Dreadnoughts, cruisers, torpedo boats and gunboat would emerge phantom-like from the southern horizon and an orderly procession would sail majestically round Proudfoot on its way to Scapa Flow.

Twice weekly would arrive the St Clair from Leith, and on occasion, her sister ship, the St Ninian, with holiday bound exiles from the south. French smacks and Dutch luggers put in an occasional appearance.

Their crews would appear in the High Street to be greeted by the budding linguists of the Academy with "Parlez vous Francais?" We knew from first hand that outside the limit the luggers carried contraband. Our year's supply of a panacea for all ills – Dutch balsam, came from them. Even at this late date, I could recall the pungent smell of that treacly liquid, which could be used internally and externally for all ailments of mankind. Accompanying each bottle were printed instructions in Dutch, which I vainly tried to translate.

There was also containers of pure Eau-de-Cologne, luggies of Dutch gin and cigars which were kept for very special occasions. These commodities, naturally, changed hands at sea and escaped the eagle eye of Customs Officials.

Unforgettable also were the elegant and graceful sailing ships, which would be seen lying at their moorings at the North Quay, their rigging network against the sky, their dazzling white and gold figureheads a fantasy of dolphins and angels, mute tributes to the craftsmen of an earlier age. When we came to Wick in the early years of the century, we came to a town where practically every local industry depended on the herring fishing. It was still the era of sail boats, but the stream drifters had begun to arrive.

The names come surging back to my memory and in my mind's eye I see the brave little craft of these days, with the sea salted heroes who sailed in them. They were, and still are, worthy of the highest appreciation and I still feel grateful that in the first year of World War I Rudyard Kipling in his "Fringes of the Fleet" paid special tribute to them.

But I make bold to say that had the same brilliant writer lived for any length of time in our grey northern town, where the sea interpenetrates so closely with the lives of men, had he known them in the years preceding its sketches, and had he became acquainted with the untiring spirit of energy and resourcefulness which with a few exceptions, pervaded all of them, he would have given us an even finer picture than he has done.

Swift to my memory comes the recollections of the summer seasons of pre-1914 days – seasons which now are enveloped in the haze of a distant far back age. For, in those of our generation, the Wick that was, died in 1914. In the years preceding World War I, life for us, as for George Borrows, gipsy hero, was very sweet."

Elizabeth Jack

The "herring days" appear in the famous Johnston photographic collection gifted to the Wick Heritage Centre. A selection are included in Iain Sutherland's interesting book: "Wick Harbour and the Herring Fishing" (1983). 1862 was the peak year at Wick: over 1000 boats were in the herring fleet, a unique and unforgettable sight.

THE MIRROR OVER THE MANTELPIECE: WICK

Mirror where sea and small ships ride
  In trance that lasts sun-up till night,
I think some shadow defied
  Endures of all your legends bright
Of what persists outside.

A room that holds life, death – and this,
  The crowded quays, the wind-chopped sea,
These million traits an eye must miss
  Observing yet – while we sip tea,
Held in our Chrysalis.

Arthur Ball
Valley of Wild Birches, 1994.

SCARBOROUGH JIMMY
THE HERMIT OF PROUDFOOT

It would be somewhere around 1910 when he first appeared in Wick, then the Herringopolis of the north – a place where the inhabitants existed because of herrings and in spite of them, for you could smell them five miles inland when the wind was blowing off the sea.

But that was before the Kaiser's war, when most of the Wick men wore dark melton trousers and navy blue jerseys, their weather-beaten faces shaded by caps usually set at a jaunty angle – that was why Scarborough Jimmy or Tudor James as we locals called him – was such an outstanding figure in the northern town which RLS called "The meanest of God's towns, on the baldest of God's bays". Tudor James, when I saw him first, was dressed in a Shepherd tartan knickerbocker suit, woollen hose and brown brogue shoes with fringed tongues hanging out. The shepherds crook stick and the collie dog on a lead, made this man with the white flowing mane, a picturesque figure in the town. He took up residence in a hut on the site of the one-time gun battery on the north headland above Wick Bay, and only visited the town to buy food and other necessities. At that time nobody seemed to know where he came from, and current speculation suggested that he was a Welshman of noble birth who was in disgrace with his family, and had been sent to this northern Burgh with a regular allowance to keep him out of the way.

It was in the early 1920's that I got to know him well – that is, as well as anyone – for he would not speak of his past or his family, gently changing the subject if it were broached. I used to take his groceries out to him on my half-day. It was a pleasant walk along the two miles of footpath that led to his windowless abode situated above the treacherous Proudfoot Reef. The path ran along the cliff top overlooking the swimming pool, past the memorial commemorating battles of long ago, and the cave where local legend says a piper played for a wager and was devoured by rats. On a Sunday afternoon in the summer, you would find Scarborough Jimmy sitting on an upturned fish box, playing and singing hymns to a group of fishermen, their navy blue suits and tanned faces a striking contrast to the green hillock on which they sat. He was a fine violinist, and although I have heard him play Schubert's "Serenade" and Brahms "Lullaby", it was mostly Sankey and Moody hymns he loved to play – hence his popularity with the fisherfolks.

He knew every fishing boat that entered and left Wick harbour, and as they steamed out into the bay, he would blow his whistle and wave a rather dirty white hat to them. When the answering call came from their siren, he would go indoors again, well pleased. His abode was packed with a varied collection of driftwood and oddments he had collected from the numerous ships that fell foul of Proudfoot Reef, and his bed was a few boards raised from the floor by a couple of fish boxes and covered by an old mattress and a few blankets. The place was lit at night by a ship's lantern. I still wonder how he did his cooking during the winter. Maybe he didn't do any, for the last meal I saw him take was a concoction of oatmeal, honey, ground coffee, brown sugar, switched egg and milk – all mixed together in an enamel bowl, observing with a twinkle in his eye that he had all the necessary calories in one meal.

He had a cat called David Livingstone, and his cockerels were all named after the famous leaders of World War I – Joffre, Clemenceau, Jellicoe and Haig, while he himself wore his peaked hat over one ear like Earl Beatty. I felt highly privileged when, on my last visit, he brought his violin out and after playing a selection from the classics, finished up with that beautiful hymn of S. Baring Gould's "Now the day is over", and as the shadows of the evening stole across the sky, the lone figure of Scarborough Jimmy waved me goodbye until out of sight.

That was a long time ago, and although the days of this lone hermit are over, it may be that in the gathering dusk above Proudfoot Reef, a wraithlike figure in a reefer jacket and peaked hat can be seen waving farewell as the ships put out to sea.

W.A. Mackay
Edinburgh Caithness Magazine.

Echo of the Herring Days, Wick.
Photographed by Dan Mackay.

The "St. Clair" at Wick Harbour. Used to sail from Leith - Aberdeen - Wick.
Photographed by Herbert Sinclair (Caithness 1925-6),

The morning sun sparkled on the sea as I sat on a grassy verge facing Wick Bay. It was an ideal viewpoint to savour the full sweep of the sea and observe the changing light on the water.

Two images emerged: pale blue to silver, with pewter grey on the Wick side. There was no wind, just the lapping tide against the rocks, and the distant cry of a gull. Tranquillity was the keynote.

Given this immense canvas of sea and sky, an artist might find inspiration or a poet picturesque lines to while away a morning, others might elect it their favourite Caithness view.

There is a mystic quality about the sea one can never really fathom, but no doubt that is part of its appeal. The sea, of course, has its beauty and its danger, a two-edged sword which north men know only too well.

Wick Bay seemed like a giant amphitheatre minus players, for save for the occasional boat, or odd seagull, the scene was quiet; only the distant hum of town life spoke of some activity.

If those rocks could speak, what might they say of the great storm of 1870 which tore the breakwater asunder or the time Prime Minister Gladstone sailed into Wick Bay on board Sir Thomas Brassery's yacht "Sunbeam", or the "Boom Century" with its armada of brown sails in the bay, its colour and bustle of harbour life?

Seafaring men struck gold along this coast in the form of herring, and it established the name of Wick for years to come, today the harvest of the sea continues in diminished form and for a different catch but the principle remains the same.

My return to Wick Bay proved a welcome interlude after the hustle of Edinburgh at Festival Time. On the North Head there was no striving for effect, only the enchantment of nature.

R.T.
John O'Groat Journal

THE SILVER DARLINGS

Tom and his crew cast their brown and green nets out over the water and knew they had a long night ahead until the next day, to see the fruits of their labours. Hot drinks were ready for the crew to keep out the biting cold of the North Sea, a little rest for some of the crew to prepare them for their tasks for the morrow.

Time to get the winch started. This was the mechanism which propelled the hawsers attached to the nets which, when pulled aboard, would disgorge the silver herrings into the hold of the trawler, where they would be kept until their return to the port where they would be put into cran baskets and emptied into the skips on the wharf, ready to

Photographed by Jane Thomson Langwill.

Echo of the Herring Days

be put onto the lorries for the fishing girls to gut from the wooden benches standing in the fish curing yard.

A few words about the herring girls; who were they? Where did they come from?

The foreman of the Fishcurer used to get lodgings for the crew as they were called, two gutters and one packer – all the girls would arrive at Wick station from the Hebrides and one could see them walking en masse from the Wick railway station through the Argyle Square Green to their various digs, carrying their suitcases. What a grand sight to see – very pretty and some delicate girls among them – and of course they all spoke the Gaelic.

The next morning they would all be getting their preparations ready for their job – tiny strips of clooties or bandages for their fingers, wrapped around with silken thread, and they would bite off the thread with their teeth as they manipulated the cotton, quite an art to do this for yourself – the reason for the protection of their fingers from the salt and the blisters from their wooden handled gutting knife to gut the herring which was extremely sharp.

These girls worked like lightning, their bodies all in rhythm bending over the bench in unison, singing the plaintive melodies of the Hebridean airs which haunted one throughout the years, long after they were all gone.

Their flashing arms glistening with the herring scales in the sunlight, would fling the gutted herrings into the plaited baskets behind them with a deadly accuracy for the packers to lift when full, and commence to pack into the clean-shaved wooden barrels, end to end and tail to tail, with the silver breast of the herring upright with a layer of salt to each tier – they had to be in perfect symmetry as the bottom tier had to be first inspected by the Cooper or Gaffer for neatness and perfection, as this would be the view the buyers would get when the barrel was opened for sale to the market.

Often you would hear the good natured girls sing out "I'm ready Jock. Bottom tier all ready for inspection", and the friendly banter would go on all day at the gutting benches. Even so, if they were not packed to perfection, the whole lot would be tipped out for the packers to start again, for you see, only perfection was the goal.

Let me tell you the rest of their attire – a scarf was tied peasant fashion over their hair to protect the hair from the salt pickle. They also wore heavy, black oilskin coats which were very stiff and only pliable when warm. The coats had two straps over their shoulders to help them carry their coats as they were quite heavy. The Baltic Boots they wore were made of leather and when the pickle soaked into them they got very stiff and the only way to soften them was to burn papers inside to give the warmth to soften before wearing; quite a performance one would say.

When there were large catches of herrings this meant that they would have to work very late into the night and they have to work with the lamps lit to gut far into the wee small hours. Then they would have to wend their weary way home to their digs and sleep the sleep of the just.

The next day one would see them all gathering at the 'Brae' sitting by the Pilot House overlooking the Wick Harbour where they would have Monday as their rest day – even then they would be furiously knitting away doing a Fair Isle pattern or knitting socks; my, my, they were grand workers these girls and their own tongue was a joy to hear, the lift of their voices speaking the Gaelic set them apart.

No doubt they would be talking about what they would do with their earnings at the end of the season. Their earnings were eightpence a barrel of herrings. The most they would get in total at the end of the fishcuring season would be a bounty of thirty pounds – what an existence and a mere pittance for such long hours of work and deprivation.

Their coming and going was a highlight and a colourful part of my youth which touched the chords of memories to enhance my own life and make me appreciate the good things I have in my own life and make me humble and content.

Alexandrina Macgregor.

SUNSET

Sea-girt tales told
  By men in dark guernseys,
With Caithness voices
  Grizzled veterans all,
Who speak a language
  Laced by the sea itself.

Men who knew Wick
  In the halcyon days,
Now cast their eye
  With a seasoned look,
As if they sought
  Another herring klondyke.

But alas, they're gone
  Those magic transient days,
When the fishing fleet
  Caught imagination
Like the morning sun.
  Now only memories remain.

There they sit on the braehead
  Like pilgrims of old,
The sea forever in their blood;
  Now their 'tale is told,
And o'er Lower Pulteneytown
  The sunset transcends all.

Ronald Thomson

The Battle of Altimarlach, which is notable for being the second last clan battle in Scotland, took place on Caithness soil on July 13th 1680.

The site of the battle, some two miles west of Wick – along the riverside – is marked by a Celtic cross which was erected in 1901. It was the idea of John (Pastor) Horne, to erect such a memorial, and his young daughter was chosen to unveil the cross at Altimarlach.

For an 11-year-old girl it was a great honour, a day to be remembered: "As it was summer, the idea was to row up the river, unveil with a speech or two and then have a picnic . . . at that time pleasure boats were on the lower reaches of the river – 6d an hour – from Mrs Groundwater, who sat in a wooden hoosie at the end of the bridge.

I see the flotilla of six or seven boats moving up the river, with their crews and passengers – the latter in summer finery. My boat came last, all male except myself, and there I sat in the stern, all starched and frilled – the joy of a mother's heart – a huge bag of apple tarts in my lap.

As the upper reaches of the river were seldom used, the weeds were apt to retard progress and it was a case of stepping overboard and pushing, but no trouble seemed to mar the sailing – I remember it so well – the loveliest day of summer sun and heat and . . . clegs!

As the river narrowed, we seemed to be moving in great fields of "Queen of the Meadow" and stalwart rushes, and as the oars lifted they were veiled with water "forget-me-nots".

Contrast that summer day with one of 220 years before: instead of a pilgrimage, imagine a battle is at hand, one which involved two clans – the Campbells and the Sinclairs.

The crux of the matter involved a disputed title, namely the "Earl of Caithness". Who was the rightful claimant?

Was it Lord Glenorchy (John Campbell) who had purchased the heritable title and lands, and whose claim had been approved by Royal Charter under the Great Seal.

Or was it – as many Caithnessians believed – that Glenorchy was an usurper, who had taken advantage of the late Earl's financial position and who "cheated him out of his title and property"?

George Sinclair of Keiss thought so, for he disputed Glenorchy's claim to the said title, and notably the lands of Northfield and Tister, which were Sinclair's inheritance. For generations the Sinclair line (Motto: "Commit thyself to God") had been the legitimate heirs to the title of "Earl of Caithness".

When Sinclair disregarded an interdict which forbade him any further claim to the Earldom, the seeds of battle were sown.

On November 11th 1679, an Act was passed which allowed Glenorchy to repossess the disputed lands. The following summer Glenorchy mustered an army – which included a detachment of the King's Soldiers – and prepared to invade Caithness.

The morning of July 13th 1680 found Glenorchy and his Highlanders wending their way toward the Burn of Altimarlach, where they lay in wait for their enemy.

According to "Calder's History of Caithness", Sinclair's men were ill-prepared for battle: they were untrained in warfare, and worse, they had consumed much liquor on the eve of the battle.

Sinclair's men advanced, while more than half of Glenorchy's army lay concealed. It was a classic ambush and the result was brief but deadly.

"The onset of the Campbells was so furious that the Sinclairs, enfeebled as they were with the debauch of the previous evening, instantly gave way and fled with precipitation in the direction of the burn of Altimarlach.

At this moment, the reserve corps of the Highlanders starting up from their ambush with a savage shout, met the fugitives in the face, and being thus pressed in front and rear, and at the same time outflanked on the left, the Sinclairs in desperation made a rush for the river.

The Campbells chased them into the water as they attempted to escape to the other side and committed such dreadful havoc that it is said they passed dry shod over the dead bodies."

The Battle of Altimarlach, violent as it was, did not last more than a few minutes. Accounts vary as to how many Caithnessians were killed. One version suggests 80, another over 200. Among the survivors was Sinclair of Keiss who escaped on horseback.

The story does not end with the debacle at Altimarlach, and the bloodshed of Sinclair's men. Ultimately, with the help of the Duke of York (later James II), Sinclair gained full possession of his patrimonial property and became Earl of Caithness. It was fitting, that summer day in 1901, that a child – the symbol of innocence – should unveil the cross at Altimarlach. For in childhood there is complete trust in God's assurances.

"And they shall beat their swords into ploughshares, and their spears into pruning hooks: nation shall not lift up a sword against nation, neither shall they learn war any more."

(Micah Chapter 4, Verse 3)

R.T., John O'Groat Journal 1975

A DAY'S JOURNEY

Blue-clouded Morven to the South, far off,
But here the wide green plain, the breathing upland
Where shadows ran and sunbeams caught the ridges
Off fresh-cut fields haunted by rook and gull.

Here I came walking. A broken wall, a gate,
A sound of trickling water. Birds
Passed me, towards the sea-cliffs of their homing,
White-winged, grey-winged: and, when I looked again,
Merging with greying distance.

Here was loneliness
Touching the earth-bound crofts, uplifting them,
Each roof, each gable-end, until the air
Loaded their austere stones with blossoming gold.

Northward, these precipices,
Sculptured by pounding storms and constant tides
Out of the rock that joins Man's war-split world.

A late thrush singing
Close to the church-yard still with truth
Made visible in loitering butterflies
On bush and grave-mound.

Then Canisbay: beyond, the island, ringed,
In dancing waves, by solitude,
Stroma, that lost her children for a dream.

Here, by the mill, I waited. This was an end
To a day's journey, here, where a stream poured
Beside bright iris-spears and meadowsweet.

Within me poured the stream, within me sang
The evening thrush.

Upon by brows the Southward mountains hung.
And as I slept the Firth would beckon me,
Scudding with blue-lit splendour, one vast jewel.

Arthur Ball.

CHAPTER 4
ALONG THE NORTH COAST

THE CAITHNESS CAT

Ah, boys, it's a great life bein' a Kaitness Cat.

My name is "Smokie" and I've spent all my nine lives on a large farm which lies about halfroads 'tween Wick an' Thirsa. The other animals hiv to work for a livin': the hens are aye layin' nice big brown and white eggs for e' workers' tea.

I've sat on e' dry stone dyke on a summer day – you know e' kind when the horizon stretches as far as my cat's eyes can see. Whiles I'm watchin' Tam out wi' e' horse and plough in the fields. Tam doffs his cap as he passes. Ah lek 'at chiel. Some others don't like cats and try to keep them out of the farm house, but I'm lucky, my master – an old chiel they call Hamish (he looks a bit like e' owl that sits in e' tree by the house) is fond o' cats. I think "Bugsna" the dog is a bit jealous, but I don't give a docken for him and his barkin'. I told him straight one day, "If you don't curb 'at barkin' I'll keep you awake in the gloaming with my caterwaullin' – an I'm famous for my caterwaullin'!" I remember once Biddy – 'ats e' elderly spinster housekeeper – threw a joog o' water out the bedroom window. Just at that moment I darted down 'e path to the rhubarb patch and Robbie, e' grizzled shepherd who was lightin' his pipe, caught the lot! Poor Robbie, he was soakin' – an' e' language! It shocked me and old Biddy.

Well, the days that followed, ye could tell there was an atmosphere. I was drinking a well-earned saucer of milk when in came Robbie with his bag of laundry. But Biddy refused to wash it. She told 'e chiel to wash it in 'e barrel outside the house.

Then Robbie made another mistake: he was shoutin' at me, "Smokie, it's a' your fault – if I get my hands on ye . . ."

Well, he chased me but I darted away, and eventually I hid in my master's bedroom. I could hear Robbie's tackety boots as he searched e' hoose. Robbie entered the bedroom. "Come oot ye vermint," sid he panting, "I'll bet he's under 'e covers." But I was under the bed and ran through Robbie's legs. On the chase went, with some shouting from Robbie; we were out-doors now. Fortunately my master appeared, saw what was happening and 'ere long brought Robbie down with a rugby tackle.

I quickly scaled e' apple tree, while down below the men continued arguing. "Either 'at cat goes or I go – take yer pick'. Hamish dusted himself down, then – "E' cat's definitely staying." Well, boys would you believe it, Robbie handed in his notice, and spoke about buying his own place. But I knew it was all a bluff. Robbie looked as if he hadn't two pennies to rub together but over the years acquired a small fortune from being thrifty. Robbie, according to gossip, mistrusted banks and stored his money in old shoe boxes under his bed.

However, to more important matters – it was milking time! I followed Biddy as she made her way to the byre carrying some large pails. Later, as I sat waiting for my share of the milk, I was joined by the usual band of stray cats. I enjoyed their company and Biddy was too busy to notice them. They say a house divided must fall, and my boss Hamish and his dog Bugsna were finding it a wearing business trying to round up the sheep for shearing without Robbie's expertise. So far Hamish had not been successful in finding a shepherd to take over Robbie's duties.

Robbie, meanwhile, I could see was struggling to hang up his washing; at times like these there always seemed to be a Kaitness gale blowing and so e' chiel lost times when his vest, long "coms" and best shirt went flying over to end up in cows' pancakes in e' next field!

The final straw for Robbie was some days later; apparently the mice had been makin' a nest of Robbie's paper money stored under his bed.

So force of circumstance brought Hamish, Robbie and Biddy round the paraffin-lit table. There was a well stacked peat fire which had turned to ashes before all parties agreed to make a new start. Proof that Robbie had turned over a new leaf was evident when the following morning Robbie patted my head and laid a portion of fish in my saucer. The sun streaked through the small window; Robbie took a chair by the open hearth and lit his pipe; I could hear Biddy callin' to my master to watch his time. Hamish brushed his boots till they were gleaming, then wearing his best navy serge suit ran up the road. E' bus was waitin'. I remembered it was Thursday, the famous market day in Wick.

I stretched, then made my way to Robbie's croft. I had a temporary post, to pursue the mice who had recently eaten part of Robbie's nest egg. . .

I don't know if Hamish got tired of travellin' in e' bus but later in the year didn't the chiel surprise us all by buying a pony called "Sandy". I sometimes watched the pony and trap set off for the town. Later I heard of their adventures, jogging through quaint narrow streets, old fisherwomen gossiping in front of shops, red faced farmers swapping yarns, punctuated by bursts of laughter, brawny fishermen coming up from the harbour. . .

At the riverside, Sandy was unharnessed, and soon was happily munching the rich green pasture while Hamish slipped away for a refreshment. . .

It was the beginning of August, boys, and I was watchin' e' blue peat smoke rising in an almost vertical spiral till it evaporated in the air while bees danced round the flowers. Round from e' back of the house came Hamish and Robbie, to where I sat on the drystone dyke. Apparently Bill Calden, our neighbour, (five miles down the road) had been bragging about his pony being the fastest animal in e' north. My boss Hamish took up the challenge and to cut a long story short arranged a great pony race for the following evening, the venue being the local post office to the village, a distance of two miles.

The news of the event quickly spread from neighbour to neighbour, and some quick searches were made for vintage field-glasses (which had seen better days) to follow the event closely. There was a sense of excitement as those interested gathered round e' post office which stood on the brow of a hill. The parties concerned lined up on a chalk drawn line. Robbie drew an aged yellow-faced watch from his waistcoat; "One minute to go lads, and good luck to all." Bill Calden nodded, while Hamish, a bit flushed looking, pulled on his best homburg – perhaps he thought his best hat added dignity to the affair. With a sudden jolt the race had begun! A cheer went up from young and old, and some caps were thrown in the air. Down the long brae went Sandy, like a horse who has found his destiny. It was a close thing though, and as the road began to narrow, on the gigs went, over the hump-backed bridge, then on, sharp right to level ground. "Come on Sandy," shouted Hamish hoping to maintain the narrow lead, but their moment of glory was brief; in a flash Bill Calden's gig was alongside – then into the lead.

Hamish could scarce believe his eyes, he had been so absorbed that he was scarcely aware of what had happened. Grabbing the whip he cracked it above Sandy's head; still the gap grew to Hamish's dismay. . .

Through the swirling dust of his gig, Bill Calden triumphantly waved! The gallant Sandy still managed a steady pace, though lagging at the halfway mark. They'll have to slow down here, thought Hamish. He was right, for they had reached the crossroads to the village. "Whoa there, Roger," shouted Bill as he drew in the reins of his pony. Sparks flew as the wheels of the gig bit the ground. . .

Less than a mile to the village! Now at last Hamish's faith in Sandy was proving true – nearer and nearer the village began to grow in size. Hamish had a determined look on his face. Faster and faster the wheels spun. Hedges and fields seemed to flash in a blur. Shades of "Ben Hur"! As they came near to the home stretch, the back of Hamish's yellow gig almost vanished through clouds of dust. There was the drumming of hooves, the rattle of wheels – who actually won the great pony race I cannot tell. Hamish stopped relating his story to light his pipe, Biddy glanced up at the mantelpiece clock – "It's time to milk the cows," and left Hamish to conclude his story to Robbie the shepherd.

E' Kaitness Cat, left with Biddy – because as far as Smokie was concerned a story is just a story – but a saucer of fresh milk is bliss.

Alan and Ronald Thomson
Lifeline Magazine – 1987

PEACE

The stars are gold in a blue velvet sky –
    The silver moon casts a path on the sea;
Towering sand dunes throw friendly shadows,
    A lone gull circles, wild and free.
Incessant breakers flowing inward –
    Maybe from some distant land,
Roll, then break, and docile whirling,
    Curl, foam speckled, on the sand.

A startled otter scurries homeward –
    The gull has gone. Now all is quiet;
Only the breakers' rhythmic music
    Disturbs the stillness of the night;
Barefooted now, I wander on –
    Sand still warm from heat of day;
All around is peace and solitude –
    Heaven can't be far away.

Miles of sand, white-gold in moonlight,
    Silver paths upon the sea;
Sand dunes towering, sea-gulls whirling –
    They're calling now, they're calling me!
Now you know why my thoughts wander,
    Why my soul can find release –
In that earth lent piece of heaven,
    All is quietness, – all is peace.

Jessie Stewart
Sinclair's Bay is the inspiration for this poem.

MAGIC OF CAITHNESS

The full sweep of the Bay revealed Caithness at her best: from Keiss on the one hand to Noss Head on the other; the rich tang of the sea, healthful and invigorating; the summer tide attractive under morning sunlight; all within walking distance from our holiday venue – "Stain" croft.

The croft was a step back in time: there was no modern convenience, save for the calor-gas stove mother cooked upon. Illumination was by paraffin lamp and candles, and drinking water had to be fetched from a neighbour's croft at the top of the road.

The croft stood within a stone's throw of Sinclair's Bay – one of the most attractive seascapes in Caithness. Few visitors came to our end of the Bay – Mother's Croft was at the foot of an unmarked cart-track, and save for an odd beachcomber, we usually had the place to ourselves.

Eye-catching were the clover fields which led to the croft, how rich and fertile they appeared – well might they inspire one of mother's poems, which conjure up the magic of Caithness.

True one missed the modern conveniences we take for granted – but once the mind accepted a more basic lifestyle – there was a sense of contentment at the croft.

Mother once remarked that each generation gets it easier than the last. And certainly the crofting-fisher folk who once inhabited "Stain" (the place of stones) must have been a hardy breed indeed.

One likes to think that the American philosopher, Thoreau, would have found "Stain" croft to his liking, for he advocated simplicity in all things, and reckoned a man was rich by the things he could leave alone.

Certainly there was time to reflect at the croft, in the relaxed tempo of holiday-time when body and spirit are being refreshed. Well might Thoreau find food for thought in the far north: time to stand and stare, time to reflect on a different way of life, for Thoreau [1], nature writer, philosopher, individualist, was above all "il penseroso" – the thoughtful man.

---

[1] *Henry David Thoreau – 1817-1862: "I learned this at least by my experiment, that if one advances confidently in the direction of his dreams, and endeavours to live the life which he has imagined, he will meet with a success unexpected "in common hours".*

THE CLOVER FIELDS OF CAITHNESS

The blue and gold of a long summer day,
  Will chase all the cares of my heart away;
When I walk on that road at the close of day,
  By the clover fields of Caithness.
By the green and cream and purple and red,
  Of the clover blooms in their grassy bed;
With the lilting song of the lark o'erhead,
  I shall be glad.
Some sigh for the flowers that the hedgerow yields,
  But give me a sight of those clover fields;
The clover fields of Caithness.

My ear will be soothed by the sound of the sea,
  And the murmuring winds on the grassy lea;
As I walk with a mind and a heart that are free,
  By the clover fields of Caithness.
By the green and cream and purple and red,
  Of the clover blooms in their grassy bed;
With the happy song of the lark o'erhead,
  There's joy to be had.
Take the scent of the rose that the hedgerow yields,
  Give to me the breath of those clover fields;
The clover fields of Caithness.

When moonlight dapples the silent bay,
  When the stars of night come out to play;
And the ground-mist is vanishing slowly away,
  By the clover fields of Caithness,
By the green and cream and purple and red,
  Of the clover blooms in their grassy bed;
With the cry of a homing bird o'erhead,
  I could not be sad.
In the pot-pourri that my memory yields,
  There's the glorious scent of the clover fields,
The clover fields of Caithness.

In the Tapestry of Life,
  Grant that there may be;
Woven with silken thread,
  Pattern of Caithness field;
With Lark o'erhead,

And clover blossoms strewn;
Like jewels on mossy bed –
Purple and Red and Cream,
Red and Cream and Purple
And Cream,
And Purple,
And Red.

Jane Thomson Langwill.

Mother had a talent for lyrical poetry, artistically, she considered "The Clover Fields of Caithness" one of her best poems. It first appeared in the Edinburgh Caithness Magazine.

Freswick district seems like a half-forgotten part of Caithness, a little world on its own, yet it lies just off the A9 Wick to John O'Groats road. Freswick is a reminder of old Caithness, a crofting-fishing community, though there is little fishing done there nowadays.

As you drive along the narrow road to Skirza Head, the eye is drawn sea-ward to Freswick Bay. A focal point is Freswick House, which stands on the margin of the Bay like a stark symbol of the past. You are now in Viking country, for Freswick was a haunt of the Norsemen, and remnants of their dwellings have been uncovered in the vicinity, also artifacts which are now in the care of the Royal Scottish Museum of Antiquities, Edinburgh.

Interesting to recall that on the south headland, the Point of Ness, stood the Norse fortress of Lambaborg, which was a stronghold of Sweyn Asliefson, who died in 1171 during a raiding expedition to Dublin.

Calder's History says that the castle had a second lease of life via the clan Mowat (who acquired the property of Freswick) and renamed it Bucholie Castle. Bucholie has long been a gaunt ruin on the Caithness coast, and what remains is said to belong to the latter era, rather than the former. It would appear that the castle was rebuilt by the Mowat family.

Mowat is a familiar name in Caithness – the Mowat family originally came from the south – but they made their home in the far north, notably at Freswick, in this quiet byway of Caithness.

THE MAGIC OF CAITHNESS

The little wild rose of Caithness is a fragile thing at best, yet how welcome it appears among the hedgerows, like an orphan of the wild. Driving back to Wick one evening I stopped to admire one or two, just about Quintfall Mains, Lyth. I knew they grew there and was pleased to see them again for they are a favourite of mine. Perhaps their isolation adds to their charm, anyway this fresh impression rekindled my thoughts on the little wild rose – the little wild rose of Caithness [1]:

Graced with gentle hue
You smile amid hedgerows,
Speak of childhood days
And that rare innocence,
Lost so long ago
Yet still held dear.

No crystal vase
Enfolds your fragrant charm,
No loving hands,
Tend your every need,
Still blest are you
Rose of the wild.

You are Nature's child
Sweet and unadorned,
Solace to the wayfarer
Along some country road,
And you touch the heart
With a memory of old.

Ronald Thomson.

THE SANDS OF REISS

Travellers journeying from Wick towards John O'Groats are irresistibly intrigued by the tantalizing glimpses of the undulating dunes and creaming breakers that fringe the glorious sandy sweep of Sinclair Bay, with the rugged headland of Noss on the one hand thrusting boldly out into the turbulent ocean, and the promontory of Keiss harbour upon the other.

It is fortunately a most gratifying experience to sojourn for a spell by the edge of the Sands of Reiss and be in constant touch with the fluctuating moods that bewitch this wonderful stretch of Caithness coastline.

An unobstructed doorstep view over the low fields and moorlands of

---

[1] *Reprinted from the Scots Magazine, and dedicated to mother, Quintfall Mains, Lyth, was where we spent our first Caithness holiday, as children in 1947.*

the remote panorama of Morven and the Scarabens, is rivalled by the broad golden band that enticingly curves away for miles to vanish at the barely distinguishable Tower of Ackergill. From day to day, every aspect of nature around the whole compass can be observed with effortless ease, and to see ever-changing glories of cloudland aflame with a riot of sunset colours – the seaward aspect reflected upon expansive waters and shining wet sands – is a vision long to be remembered.

In chastening contrast, there are a few dreary rain-sodden and mist-driven days when the sound of dripping water, the booming turmoil of storm-thrashed breakers, and the still more menacing constant blare of the Noss foghorn, make the well banked peat fire and the homely flagstone floor a very welcome refuge.

But what a joy to waken to a shining morning when the peaceful and fresh-scented world is flooded with an omniscient amber glow of unearthly beauty, gilding the commonplace features with a glory that instantly recalls the immortal lines of John Horne's poem on "Canny" that picture for us, such a Caithness morning with vivid artistry of description and deep sentiment. Over the sparkling bay, the distant cliffs of Noss stand brightly out, presenting a ruddy bulwark of broken buttresses and sharply edged shadows of goes and cletts in amazing clarity, surmounted by the ancient towers of Girnigoe, Sinclair and Ackergill that still proclaim something of their stormy history in sturdy bastions illumined by the early sunlight.

The firm and level sands provide an ideal pathway for a carefree daily stroll along the margin of the sea. Morning, noon and evening each hold their own fascination as the unceasing waves curl up and smooth out in an infinite variety of shape and sound.

Sometimes the wind shears off the tortured crests and sends the spume spinning away like a cloud of incense over the bay, and the dry surface of the upper strand becomes weirdly alive as it flows along in eddying patterns before the gusty onslaught.

As days pass by, the growing desire to traverse the entire length of the sands and reach that beckoning tower of Ackergill becomes irresistible, until at last we set off upon our venture along the lonely shore. Here, alongside the surging, colourful seas, as they pound the level beach, is surely one of the most delightful walks in the county, the firm even sands providing a perfect footway. The mind completely relaxes, entirely free from the anxiety of traffic, with the whole seaboard to ourselves to absorb unrestricted impressions as we leisurely saunter along.

Restless groups of dunlins, turnstones and sandpipers flitter around the water's edge as we approach and solemn congregations of black-backs on the outlying sandbanks suspiciously regard us, and finally launch themselves aloft in a swirling cloud of protesting cries, to reluctantly alight elsewhere. Countless bird footprints tell their own story of constant activity in search of food.

A coasting seal pops up his head, and quizzically watches us each time he surfaces. All the way the sand dunes reveal their ever-changing fantastic shapes that remind us of the vast primeval forces that fashioned our county's unique character.

Near the Wester River, two fisher-lads come down to spread their salmon nets, and soon we have to speculate how to cross the river mouth. However, it proved quite easy in bare feet across the spreading shallow outfall, and thus we continued for another mile, splashing in and out of the surge, swinging our shoes like unfettered bairnies till we pass the wreck of an abandoned drifter – grim reminder, with its rusted hulk and prostrate mast upon the strand – of tragic tempestuous nights battled on the winter seas. Presently we halt for a picnic snack beside the dunes, and marvel how Keiss seems so diminished and Ackergill so near – we are certainly getting on!

Shortly after resuming our jaunt – with respectably shod feet – we espy upon the beach ahead a solitary figure that turned out to be a lady from the far south enjoying a few hours solitude with a book, free from domestic cares, while her family were off shooting and pony riding. She was obviously delighted to relate her joy in such unwonted peacefulness and so we passed on, richer for having shared our mutual pleasures.

Another short trek, and then Ackergill Tower dominates the entire neighbourhood in amazing majesty as we leave the sands and wander round its towering battlements. Truly this mighty edifice in all its magnitude and history, is a fitting termination to such a glamourous journey.

We reach the highway, to rejoin the world of speed and urgency and return elated in the knowledge that to us the Sands of Reiss are no longer shrouded in the realms of mystery. A last lingering memory is of a twilight evening stroll along the darkening sands, when the red light of Noss flares out rhythmically, the lights of Keiss spring up, the stately herons flap silently down upon the wrack-strewn boulders of Stain to keep their dusky vigil.

The landward aspect is spangled with the scattered lights of remote steadings, and the roving beams of journeying cars, bound one knows not whither.

George McLeod.

Above article from the 1960 issue of the Edinburgh Caithness Magazine. Editor of Magazine 1955-1959.

MAGIC OF CAITHNESS

Imagine a choice morning in Caithness, the open road inviting under sunlight, and all the freedom of holiday time! Where to travel – strike inland, or seek out an intriguing part of the coastline?

For something unusual, try the stacks of Duncansby which are in the John O'Groats area, yet far enough away from that tourist venue.

Take the Duncansby lighthouse road to the car park and then proceed to those eye-catching stacks on foot. It's not a long walk but distant enough for a post-breakfast stroll along the grassland which leads to the famous stacks, impressive pieces of cliff scenery.

One writer likened them to the Gothic spires of a cathedral, triangular shaped, they are strangely symbolic of Caithness and are most notable viewed from the shoreline.

Historian Calder praised Duncansby Head: "But by far the most beautiful promontory on the coast of Caithness is Duncansby Head". He admitted it was a small headland compared with Dunnet, but in his opinion it had greater interest.

Calder records that near the top of the promontory, there once stood the ancient fort of Dungalsbae, the earliest stronghold of the Scandinavian Earls of Orkney and Caithness. Nothing of this remains.

Although Duncansby Head is only a few miles from John O'Groats, there is a feeling of remoteness in this corner of Caithness where the rough hewn stacks seem like sentinels, under the great dome of sky.

MY FAVOURITE VIEW

The choice of any favourite view must, as a matter of course, depend largely on personal preference, on associations, and memories. Most of us have a great love for the place we were born in, or at least brought up in, and this would seem to apply particularly to Caithnessians and their home county.

To me, the appeal of Caithness lies in the grandeur of the rock scenery, the rocks forming a barrier holding in check the ever-changing sea; and the moor, locally known as "the hill" rolling away to the horizon in colours varying from darkest grey through shades of purple, to a glowing wine-red in the rays of the setting sun. A profusion of wild flowers, for which Caithness is famous, adds to the colourful charm of the roadside ditches and the grassy stretches along the shore.

But to come nearer. Stand with me at the top of the Hill of Harley, having come up from Freswick and Skirza, and see how the gentle rise of the land from the hill here extends to the western horizon on the one hand and to the east to Noss Head, crowned by its brilliant white lighthouse. To the west, one can see far across the county and I am reminded of the old lady who many years ago told me that "12 parishes can be seen from the nearby hillag".

Maybe she exaggerated a little, but certainly one can see to the land around Dorrery.

From Noss Head, the whole stretch of Sinclair Bay runs in to the Links of Wester and Keiss – and what a wonderful bay it is. The rocky parts of the shore are "girdled with castles from ancient days", three great, grim ruins, Girnigoe, Sinclair and Keiss, with brochs interspersed, reminding us of the people of the past, all the shore carpeted with primroses, seapinks or green berry heather, according to the time of year.

This is a panorama unsurpassed by any other Scottish view, be it mountain, forest or valley. Seagulls wheel and skirl overhead and the lapwing makes its mournful cry further inland, the only sounds apart from the noise of the sea, sometimes no more than a murmur, when the surface looks like a vast sheet of pewter, at other times sparkling blue and silver with the black seals or porpoises shearing through the water, a sight to be remembered and stored in the archives of memory.

Reflecting the grey of the sea, one may look in vain for a sky of unclouded blue, as the grey clouds hang, an impenetrable curtain between us and the sun. But today, we have been lucky.

Great patches of blue, merging into a haze towards the horizon, with

Lyth Country Scene.
Photographed by Jane Thomson Langwill.

soft white fleecy clouds floating away high up, and casting their shadow on the green and brown countryside. So today we may see the land at its best. Come nearer to the great expanse stretching to the blue mountain border to the south.

All around us lies the arable land, green in spring, but golden yellow at harvest, with the various farmsteads here and there, instilling a wonderful sense of peace.

One has a deep feeling of fellowship with the folk of the district, warm-hearted kindly men and women, seldom effusive but ever welcoming. Meeting them brings back memories of schooldays and gives meaning to the natural beauty around and indeed supplies an essential element in our appreciation of the scene.

Maybe this is not a beautiful view in the conventional sense, as Jimmy MacGregor recently remarked about another Scottish view, maybe not typical Scottish scenery but nevertheless a scene of quiet restful beauty, and most dear home.

Miss M.A. Roloff.

The above article was awarded third prize in the Alan Thomson Memorial Competition.

JOHN O'GROATS

There is a strange fascination for man in the idea of a place which is the end of things. Is not the whole history of world-exploration a history of the human desire to "compass the ends of the earth"? And not only in the physical realm but in the poetic, too. "Beyond the horizon's brim" lies the garden of the Hesperides, or the more magical (to A Gael, anyway) Tir nan Og, land of the ever-young; "marvellous land, full of music, where the hair is primrose yellow and the body white as snow. . . and the hue of the foxglove is on every cheek." So to the scientist, mathematician, philosopher – a reaching out to an end, an ultimate. Without as much, how stagnant, sterile, life would be!

Yet so constantly a "striving and a striving and an ending in nothing" does the ambition prove itself, so often does the end turn to ashes or, at best, be recognised but as the first step in an endless aspiring, that unless man were fronted by some incalculable destiny, surely he would have grown tired of the game long, long ago; grown tired and cynical, and died.

World-old reflections, perhaps, that yet have a certain warmth of life when, for the first time, on a clear sunny day, you top the last ridge of Caithness county and look down on the land of John O'Groats. In that first glimpse there is something of the magic of at least transient fulfilment, as though desire did at last manage to taste of its own dream. There is the last rim of the mainland, and beyond it the blue, blue sea, and set in the sea surely the Isles of the Blest! Truly a touch of enchantment rendered breathless by a faint incredulity. You turn your back, hoping the human, if mostly foolish, hope that the "first fine rapture" may be recaptured in a second glimpse – suddenly to find that this grey flat land of Caithness you have been driving through, treeless, stone-diked, or fenced with great slate flags, has magically developed a mysterious charm, a breadth of atmosphere, a wonder of its own, that appeals as old tales of the clans and the Norsemen appeal, as sagas and poems of Ossian. For the prospect is now unquestionably on the grand scale, compelling, magnificent. Indeed, it may well be that from no other spot in these islands can such a sense of illimitable horizons be obtained. A bare 400 feet above sea level, yet the whole county stretches from your feet like a single moor, till a limit is set to it by Morven, that lodestar of Caithness fishermen, and the Sutherland peaks standing against the horizon like little cones. Southward the eye sweeps the whole extent of the Moray Firth, and imagines it can trace very faintly the dim outlines of the Moray hills on the other side. A complete history of the Moray Firth as a fertile fishing ground, embracing the habits, customs, and dress of the numberless generations of fishermen who have inhabited its creeks and harbours, would, I often think be as fascinating and romantic a history as could well be written. Eastward the Moray Firth widens, merges, and gets lost in the North Sea, and in a moment the eye is baffled by the meeting of sea and sky in that faint line that is like the closing of mysterious lips. Then, suddenly turning back again, turning northwards, behold the blue waters once more, and the islands of the Orkneys and Stroma Isle set in the blue waters!

It is difficult to refrain from phantasy should one happen to look on the Pentland Firth on a day of flying wind and sun. Even on the calmest day the waters are always in turmoil, sweeping their restless tidal way at anything from six to 10 miles an hour, west or east, to the raging "Men of Mey" or to the devouring "Bores of Duncansby", those tumultuous collisions of cross currents; but with sun behind one and the wind blowing, how intensely blue the colour, how white the tossing manes of the sea-horses, glistening, gleaming! It becomes easy to see how myth and legend found beginnings, how folk-lore and strange traditions thrived, and, what perhaps appeals more, how beginnings had necessarily to be born out of the stuff of heroism. Lives spent between those surging waters and this grey land had to be cast in a strong mould, and the bards' tales of their heroes, mythical or otherwise, had to be of a nature that inspired to deeds of endurance and courage and daring.

The thought sends the eye of its own accord across the Pentland, seeking nor'-west for the Brough of Birsay, which lies a little to the north of that visible headland of Hoy, standing so starkly there, its face to the west. Somewhere off the fatal brough one night in June 1916, in a storm-ridden sea, the Hampshire went down. . . The bards and the skalds, in the old sense, are dead, perhaps, but the old wonder and fear are still native to the heart, and who knows what "myth" the historian of a thousand years hence may have to "explain away"?

So one looks at the islands more curiously. Midway in the channel is the bare but picturesque-looking island of Stroma. It is not one of the Orkney group, and comes under the jurisdiction of the parish of Canisbay, in which John O'Groats is situated. For anyone with a whole day to spend, a row or a sail across (weather being suitable – which, alas! is the exception), and an exploration of the manifold points of interest, makes a memorable excursion. Bearing about nor'-east, Skerry Lighthouse flashes in the sun like a white marble column, looking a very fairylike guard this fair day for the "Stormy Pentland". Then, stretching right and left, bounding the horizon in front, are the southern Orkneys. Rock-bound they look, raising their walls out of the water not unlike gargantuan battleships, anchored with that grey immobility that suggests titan power. A certain entrance is pointed out to you, the entrance to Scapa Flow. Scapa Flow, the *Hampshire*. . . Suddenly you realise the sheer ancient and modern national importance of this "end of things". Galley and Dreadnought, Viking and War Minister: History repeats herself, however dressed for the occasion; the line of endeavour is continuous, and the heroic soul is still the heroic soul.

The famous traditional John O'Groats House is now nothing but a green mound, and to the present generation the name images little beyond white gleaming sands, where one hunts endless hours for the beautiful "John O'Groats buckies", and the modern hotel with its "every convenience", from garage to wine cellar. There is a room in this hotel, which, on your remarking as to its somewhat curious shape, will possibly be the means of calling forth the story of the strange building of that house which is now the green mound, the house that has succeeded in giving its interesting name in perpetuity to this end of the world. The story, or tradition, as I have heard it, varies in the telling, but the generally accepted version is that given, I understand, by Dr Morison in his *Old Statistical Account of Canisbay*. It is a very human story, not without its parallel in more famous corners of world history. Stated briefly, it runs somewhat like this:

Three brothers, natives of Holland, Malcolm, Gavin and John de Groat, came from the south of Scotland to Caithness during the reign of

James IV, with a letter from that Scottish monarch recommending them to the countenance and protection of his loving subjects in the county. They obtained lands in the parish of Canisbay, either by purchase or royal charter, and in the course of time so throve that there came to be eight different proprietors of the name of Groat. To commemorate the date of their arrival in the county, they established an annual feast, and on one such festive occasion the inevitable dispute arose on the all-important question of precedence. (Highland enough, these Dutchmen! though not possessing, it appears, the perfect aplomb of the chieftain who, in somewhat similar circumstances, dismissed the matter with the magnificent gesture: "Wherever the Macpherson sits, that's the head of the table!"). John de Groat, now far on in years, settled what looked like the development of an ugly dispute by the cunningest interference and advice. In a voice full of the wisdom and toleration of the aged, he pointed out how well off they were in matters of worldly gear in this the land of their adoption; how fratricidal strife would leave them open to the attack of their enemies and would inevitably be their undoing; and how, if they would but behave themselves on the present occasion and go quietly home, he would guarantee them a satisfactory solution of the difficulty at the next meeting (for he was wise enough to know that advice alone rarely achieves human ends).

Having so persuaded them, the worthy John forthwith set about the erection of a house that would have eight walls, eight windows, and eight doors; and when in due course the octagonal house was completed, he placed inside it an oak table with eight sides. At the next meeting each entered by his own door and sat at an unquestionable head of the table; and so enchanted were they all with this most equitable arrangement that the old harmony was restored. Thus, like the Arthurian Round Table, came into existence John O'Groats House (though it would seem, indeed, the wily Dutchman could have given points to the illustrious knights!).

One other explanation of the name may be given. It is certainly an ingenious one, and mentioned by Robert Mackay in his *History of the House of Mackay* as being traditional, though Calder, the Caithness historian, has been unable to find, he states, any such tradition in the country. Here it is:

John, a ferryman plying between Orkney and Caithness, had frequent disputes with his passengers about the fare, till in the end the magistrates took up the matter and fixed the charge at fourpence, or one groat, per head. Thereafter the ferryman was called Johnny Groat, and thus became the ancestor of the whole Groat family.

For devastating simplicity it certainly takes some beating, and if a libel on the house of Groat – or, in other words, a manufactured "tradition" – it all goes to show that the ways of the heathen Chinee in that which is "childlike and bland" were not unknown to some derisive clansman bent on putting "interloping foreigners" in their place!

One further and naively irresistible thing about this old house was recorded by the late "Cairndhuna" in one of his interesting northern articles to the *John O'Groat Journal*, as having been extracted by him from the inside cover of the visitors' book "kept an old-world hospice at Huna". Below a representation of the arms of the Groat family is the date 1839 and some writing, from which the following: "It is stated in Chambers's *Picture of Scotland*, 3rd edition, volume 2, page 306, that the foundations or ruins of John O'Groats House, which is perhaps the most celebrated in the whole world, are still to be seen."

In history of a more or less northern importance, the vicinity of John O'Groats has been necessarily embroiled to a very great extent. Every small ferry in the Highlands has its own local history and traditions, but John O'Groats represented the landing-spot on the mainland for the Norse Earls of Orkney – and was, so to speak, an international ferry. According to a remote tradition it was in striving to reach this spot that the Picts were lost in the Pentland Firth, after having been first driven to the Orkneys by the victorious Scots, and then back again by the Orcadians; whence arose the name itself – Pictland or Pentland Firth. But two historical happenings of a much wider appeal may be mentioned; and for appropriate quotations reference has been made to that admirable *History of Caithness* by Calder (first published, 1861).

The first throws a certain very interesting light on what might be called the brighter side of soldiering under Cromwell, or, to quote Calder, "Cromwell's soldiers are represented in history as rigid sectaries of the most austere cast, to whom everything in the shape of amusement, and especially on the Lord's day, was a heinous sin and an abomination, but it would seem that such of them at least as came to John O'Groats were not so very strict."

He arrives at this conclusion after quoting some entries from the old session record of Canisbay, which would point to an occupation by Cromwellian troops on three separate occasions. The first on 29th March, 1652: "No session holden by reason the Inglishe were quartered in the bounds; the congregation was few in number, and there was not a sederunt of elders, nather was ther any delinquents." Again on 2nd May, 1652: "There not being a sederunt, by reason of a party of Englishe horsemen being in our fields, whilk make the congregation fewer in number, and severall of the elders to be absent." And finally, that which gives to so much reading between the lines, on 30th December, 1655: "Adam Seaton convict of drinking on the Sabbathe, and having masking plays in his house for the Inglishe men, he was ordained to make publick confession of his fault next Sabbathe."

The second instance, which will appeal to students of Scottish history, and perhaps particularly to sympathisers, poetic or otherwise, with the Jacobite cause, has to do with the gallant Montrose. When he crossed over from Orkney with a body of men, it was in the vicinity of John O'Groats that he landed on that last fateful attempt of his to win a throne for a Stuart. Three flags he unfurled – two for the king, and one of his own, with the motto which so significantly sums up the character of the man – *"Nil Medium"*. Or, to translate it into his own quatrain:

> He either fears his fate too much,
> Or his deserts are small,
> That dares not put it to the touch
> To gain or lose it all.

Montrose lost it all at Carbisdale in the spring of 1650, and fled the stricken field, only to meet his end at the hands of his enemies at the Cross in the High Street of Edinburgh, in a manner surely brutal and heathenish enough to accord ill with their sanctimonious professions.

Neil M. Gunn.
Chamber's Journal (1925).

John O'Groats is 875 miles from Land's End in Cornwall – the greatest distance between any two points on the British mainland – however, Dunnet Head, has the distinction of being the most northern point on the mainland with the Lizard in Cornwall its counterpoint in the south.

Stroma: The name is as compact as the island itself – the only one in the Pentland Firth which belongs to Caithness. The old Norse name "Straumsey" means "the island in the current" and a strong force it is which drives the Firth.

In Calder's day the island contained about 200 people, who depended on fishing for their livelihood. Today the island is a ghost one, save for visits by its owner, Mr James Simpson, who is a Caithness farmer, and the occasional visitor.

Stroma's size, some two miles by one mile, and its location in the stormy Pentland Firth, coupled with the disappearance of fish from the range of local boats, and crofting not being viable on its own, were factors which contributed to depopulation, and those who sought the mainland began an exodus which proved irreversible.

In Calder's day, there was a school but no church on the island and when the weather was fair Stroma folk came to worship at Canisbay

Kirk. My great grandfather, was one of the Caithness men who helped to build the church on Stroma, a worthy task indeed.

Stroma has a rugged coastline, dangerous in places, where the relentless sea has made inroads in the 100 foot cliffs; those "glupes" are a key feature on the island. Stroma is a fertile island, rich with wild flowers, and notable for its bird life; a place of memories and dreams where the bright light of its lighthouse remains like a guardian of old.

A fascinating episode in Stroma life came with the "Floating Shops" – an enterprising Orcadian fitted several boats with provisions for sale to the islanders – it was a two-way business, for Stroma folk sold fish, lobsters and eggs to the merchants.

Margaret Aitken, a former resident of Stroma, writes engagingly about these "Floating Shops" with information from her grandmother, and a friend, Mr James Allan. The boats (a little fleet of sailing smacks, were attractively titled; "Star of Bethlehem", "Summer Cloud", "Glenear", "Star of Hope" and "Endeavour". Not only Stroma was served but Orkney and Shetland too.

The "Star of Hope" called once a fortnight, throughout summer, at the north end of Stroma; while the "Endeavour" visited the south side of the island each alternate week. The following recollection centres on the "Star of Hope": "At the sight of her white sails approaching from the Orkneys, the word was passed round. "The floating shop's coming!" was the signal for various preparations to be made, for she came not only to sell but to buy.

The womenfolk gathered eggs into white enamel pails and lidded baskets. Fishermen set about preparing what they called "the wet fish". At this time of year when the fish were plentiful and the market limited for disposing of fresh catches, a method of pickling was used.

On the boats' return from sea, possibly late in the evenings, the fish were cleaned, split, boned and washed in fresh water. Then, after being allowed to drip for a few minutes, they were laid, layer about with salt, in a barrel. In about three days' time the fish were floating in salt pickle.

When the floating shop was sighted the fish were swished about in the pickle to remove any sliminess, piled up, covered with canvas and a large stone was placed on top to press out the water. Then, in barrows and baskets, they were taken to the shore and loaded into the boats.

Boxes of lobsters were also put aboard, and from as far as John O'Groats and Mey on the Caithness coast local boats brought their catch.

By the time the "Star of Hope" reached her anchorage at the north end, the pier there was crowded with people from every part of the island.

The fishermen, with their boatloads for sale, were ready to go out to the ship. The other customers settled down to wait their turn to be ferried out, three or four at a time, in the floating shop's own small rowing boat.

The floating shop had three of a crew, and each man was in charge of a department. Nearest the bow of the ship was the grocer at his counter.

Along the bulkheads and sides of the ship were shelves on which the groceries were displayed. Bars of wood were nailed in front of the goods to prevent them tumbling off the shelves. Midships there was kept the meal and feeding stuffs.

A large weighing machine stood in the centre, and sacks of flour, oatmeal, bere meal, bran and Indian corn were built up along the sides.

The least busy of the departments was nearest to the stern – the drapery. The draper had his goods set out on a bench right round his domain, as well as on barred shelves and hanging on criss-cross lines above his head. When a lull came, and no-one wanted a pair of boots, a roll of wallpaper, an overall or oilskin, it didn't mean he could relax. He was expected to jump on deck and deal with the incoming lobsters and fish.

He counted the lobsters, paid out 1s or 1s 2d for each, and packed them in the ship's own boxes. These, when full, he dumped overboard to keep the supply fresh and alive until the ship was ready to leave.

The fish he weighed on deck giving about 8s to 10s per hundredweight, and then stacked them and covered them over with canvas.

The grocer bought in the dozens of eggs a 6d per dozen, and packed them between layers of straw in large boxes. Part of his duties took him on deck too, for he was responsible for the casks of paraffin lashed there.

The three men must have a hard working five hours or so in their often hot, rather cramped premises. Frequently too there was a strong rolling motion to endure – the cause of considerable discomfort to some of the women customers.

At the end of the day's business the hatches were closed, mainsail set, anchor heaved in, and foresail hoisted. Usually this was carried out as uneventfully as the putting up of shutters in a quiet street. On one occasion, however, this was not so.

As the "Star of Hope" lay at anchor, the wind changed and was beating hard on shore when she tried to leave. The man working the hand winch to heave the anchor aboard was suddenly knocked unconscious by a snapped pinion from the anchor windlass.

Fortunately the local boatmen, as was their custom, had stayed to help with the heaving of the anchor. The injured man was cared for, and then the little boats towed the ship round until her head was turned offshore and her sails able to catch the wind.

Stroma enjoyed this service from about 1910 to the Great War, and for a few years after 1918 it was resumed with engine-driven ships.

But as early as 1897 the girl who was to become my grandmother, filled huge wooden boxes with boots, bales of men's shirting, wool and the half-bleached cotton, ladies used for making their underwear.

It must often have seemed a tiresome way to earn her weekly 6s and realise the distant dream of a hat trimmed with roses. Would it have lightened the task had she known she was helping to stock the Aladdin's cave of many another girl?"

Margaret Aitken.
Reprinted from the Scots Magazine.

It was raining, and the wind was rising when I reached Huna, some miles nearer John O'Groats, and I stood in the lee of a shed while John Sinclair's open boat was made ready for the crossing to the Island of Stroma which defies the terrible tides of the Pentland Firth. John had lost a leg early in life, and he used a crutch in place of it. I was fascinated by the way he got around, under extremely difficult conditions, for in spite of his handicap he never made a slip. The crutch, by long use, had taken the place of his missing leg. He was a remarkable man, for he had to take his boat across the most dangerous channel in the British Isles, and his knowledge of the terrible rip-tides of the Pentland Firth was unsurpassed. For many years he had been the link between Stroma and the mainland.

We crossed the Inner Sound, about two miles wide, without trouble, and I spent most of a wet and windy day with the island's minister, the Rev. R. D. Maclennan. The rain continued, and the wind kept rising as I explored the island. We were joined by Mr W. A. Bremner, a crofter. He was very anxious to show me the nest of a peregrine falcon, so we walked towards the north end of the island until we reached the brink of a gigantic gash in the cliffs called Ramigoe. We crawled down into a grassy pocket at the very edge of the cliff, from which we could look down into the precarious nest of the falcon. It contained two young birds. Sea-birds, in countless thousands, were clinging to every foothold on the great cliff, so the falcon's nest was well sited. Far below, the sea crashed and writhed against the rocks.

"Just look at it!" said Mr Bremner, and he did not need to say any more, for the endless battle waged by the Pentland Firth seas against Stroma creates blood-chilling whirlpools like the one called "Swelkie". The cliff where we crouched was at least 200 feet high, but in the great storm which struck the Pentland Firth in the winter of 1862, the seas rose above it and swept right across the island.

From the base of that cliff a tunnel had been bored by the sea to the centre of the island, where it ended in a vast unfenced crater of great depth called the Glupe. We walked over to it. Green sea water was churning at the bottom of the awesome hole, for the wind was still rising. When a real storm develops, the roar of the Glupe can be heard a mile away, and its imprisoned water sends up a spray which drifts across the island like smoke.

The rain drove across the island, the wind rose to gale force, and mist obscured the coast of Caithness.

"You won't get back today", said the minister, but he walked down to the pier with me to make sure.

"Just as I thought, nobody here!" he said.

We walked back to John Sinclair's croft. John was working in a shed but he hobbled around the house and had a good look at the Sound.

"You really want to cross today?" he asked.

"Well, yes, if it is possible", I replied. – "I haven't as much as a toothbrush with me'.

"We'll try it", said John.

Twenty minutes later we were out in the Sound, bucking an ebb tide which was opposed by the gale. I have made some rough crossings to our small islands in open boats, but I have never seen such waters as those we went through between Stroma and Huna that day. The tumbling rapids of the first tidal bore, rushing through the Sound at 10 knots, seemed to stop our boat dead at times, hoisting it to the summits of great piles of angry water, then sending it reeling down at a dizzy angle into the troughs. I am not easily scared at sea, but our first contact with that dangerous bore made me hold my breath, and I thought of something the minister told me earlier in the day.

"There is one thing we newcomers learn here", he said. "So far as the outside world is concerned, we are in the hands of John Sinclair and his crew, and they never let us down". They didn't let me down, and the last I saw of John Sinclair, he was getting aboard his boat again from a slippery pier, and doing it confidently with the help of that crutch.

John Herries McCulloch.
The Charm of Scotland (published 1960).

Further reading: "Stroma" – Edited by Donald Young, North of Scotland Newspapers (1992).

Canisbay Kirk – Memorial Site of Jan de Groot.

Photographed by Ronald Thomson.

SONG OF CANISBAY

A song – a wild and rousing strain,
  From the very heart of me;
With all the passion and the pain,
  And music of the sea.
The sea that beats around the coast,
  And washes up the bay;
Of gallant vessels wrecked and lost,
  On the coast of Canisbay.

I've seen the sullen waters boil,
  I've seen them swiftly leap;
Around old Stroma's rocky Isle,
  Like a monster fast asleep!
I've stood to watch a treacherous calm,
  On a cloudless summer's day;
When the ocean chanted its quaint psalm,
  On the shores of Canisbay.

My heart is great with memory,
  Yet not unmixed with pain;
Of Huna Inn beside the sea,
  And nights of wind and rain.
Of stories of the Pentland Firth,
  And worthies passed away;
Whose ashes in their native earth,
  Repose in Canisbay.

Henry Henderson – The Bard of Reay (1873-1957).

CAITHNESS: LASTING IMPRESSIONS

Is there life north of Inverness? Before I made my first journey to Caithness in September 1980 to serve as the minister of the church in Canisbay, many individuals seemed anxious to convince me that the land north of the River Ness was virtually uninhabited and most certainly barren. "You're not going to **live** up there are you?" they would protest. "There's nothing north of Inverness". And so when I set off by bus on a clear September morning from the Inverness bus station, my destination Wick, I was apprehensive to say the least.

The journey between Inverness and Wick takes three to four hours by car, but the Highland Omnibus, no doubt keen to give its patrons ample opportunity to view the landscape, stretches this pilgrimage into eight

77

or nine hours. By the time I arrived in Wick still clinging to my seat after the bus driver's casual but competent handling of the steep roads around Berriedale, it was dark. After a welcome by a waiting minister, we drove out to Huna where I was to spend my first night in Caithness. No sooner had we left Wick than I experienced for the first time the fog that can sweep in so quickly off the coast and smother the countryside like a damp, misty blanket. When we arrived in Huna and got out of the car, the only sound of welcome was the mournful tone of a foghorn. Through the milky night I could just make out the occasional blur of a lighthouse beacon or the lights of a farmhouse. Around me on every side was the silence that can be spoken by open spaces. The waves lapped gently against the Huna pier. This was Caithness.

I will never forget my first morning in the "land of nothing" north of Inverness. How wrong had my acquaintances been! In this northern most part of Britain's mainland, the nothing of my expectations was transformed into the everything of unlimited horizons and shades of browns, greens and blues. The family with whom I spent my first night in Caithness and who would be my hosts and adopted family for the rest of my 10-month stay in Canisbay, revealed to me the land. It was a fertile wilderness of uninhibited space where land, sea and sky formed a great loving hand which held us in its palm. Everywhere was space, and everywhere was the wind. From my host's kitchen window in Huna I caught my first glimpse of Stroma, and beyond it, the Orkneys. These islands looked to me as though some northern giant had thrown massive green clods of fertile earth into the Pentland Firth to serve as stepping stones for some journey he might make to the far north. To the west, nestled in a slight hollow of the land, lay the church. Beneath the blue sky of the morning and the haze of the sea air, it shone white, and seemed to rest quietly amidst the invisible spirit of the wind and the grass of the pastures that waved and played in the breezes. Even from a distance I felt that the church was a sanctuary among sanctuaries: a heart of the community which lay in a greater heart of spirit and sky that embraced all of us in that vast, open space.

What most impressed me about Caithness during my first days there was the sense of living in landscape that always beckoned my gaze towards the farthest horizon. I felt very deeply too, that it was a land fertile with contrasts; sea and sky, moor and farmland; remote inland lochs and small cities which had evolved around harbours. Living in Canisbay I felt a greater sense of communion with the wider world than I had ever experienced while living in cosmopolitan American cities. I imagined the watery cousins of those waves which rushed against the cliffs of Dunnet Head lapping gently onto beaches along the Indian Ocean or South China Sea. The Gulf Stream not only brought warmth but carried a constant cargo of small shells from the Gulf of Mexico which it deposited like a gift offering on the sands of Duncansby Head near John O'Groats. And rainbows seemed to stretch from Denmark out to the Faeroes, bridges of colour so immense in their arc that they touched and even disappeared into the vault of the heavens. And strolling along any one of the long hems of white sand by the Caithness coast I imagined I could feel the great curve of the globe under my feet and before my eyes.

There is something about the human soul which requires solitude, and in Caithness, even in towns like Thurso or Wick, or Halkirk, it is possible to find a mood that nourishes the contemplative in all of us. Those skies of the north that can be filled with endless blue or dinosaurs of puffy, white clouds, or approaching storms the colour of steel, made it possible for me to realise how near and sustaining are the mysteries of life. On open moors, at the harbour in Wick in the midst of its great heritage of men that go down to the sea in ships, and along Dunnet sands, I learned solitude and was taught that life is as free and vibrant with energy as the Caithness landscape. I learned to listen and in the rich silence created by wind, the roaring of the sea, and the ordinary bustling and conversation of people in their unique dialect, the sounds of Caithness listened to me. As I visited people in the congregation throughout Gills and Freswick and John O'Groats, I was alone often enough to feel under my feet that unique sweep of land and sea that some refer to as "nothing". But for me it became everything: mother earth, sister sea and brother sky. Somehow the cries of cormorants and the blooming of the bog cotton were sufficient nourishment for a wandering soul from a foreign country.

Caithness is a wilderness because it forces us back upon the sheer immensity and power and staggering detail of creation and the care of the creator that shaped and continues to hover lovingly over what is minuscule as well as what is mighty. But Caithness is a fertile wilderness because its good earth can be so rich, its people so welcoming, and its associations so vivid in the memories of those who have left it for other fertile wildernesses. It is a place which stills the soul. Caithness, more than any other place I have lived in, lives inside me. It is as though its silence and the voices of its inhabitants, its awesome beauty and penetrating winds, created a space within me where I might always be nourished and inspired by the truth and beauty represented by that corner of the world. And perhaps most importantly, Caithness is a place where people still know how to listen and look. It is a tapestry of rich speech and colourful creation and where the miracle of what is ordinary and human can blossom before whom ever would take the time to stand alone before the eye of the northern skies, and be embraced by the restless wind.

Rev. E. Horstmann.
Edinburgh Caithness Magazine.

HERITAGE

Striding up the old roadie at morning,
 With the heavenly air in the face;
Every turning a rich benediction,
 Every landmark still tinctured with grace;
There's a theme in the purl of the burnie,
 Like the lilt in the heart all the way;
And the roadside is jewelled with floorags,
 Up the strath from the sweep of the bay.

Climbing up the clifftops at noontide,
 While the clamorous gulls throng the cletts;
Far below wheel the fulmars and solans,
 Salmon fishers ply round to their nets;
Tracking ships smudge the silver horizon,
 Gleams and gloomings in endless array;
Caithness garland of motion and colour,
 Is adorning the brow of the day.

Tramping over the tracks on the moorland,
 Lying wreathed in the westerly glow;
Distant mountain and dhu-loch and peat moss,
 Watching down on the ocean flow;
Stepping onwards and up to the hilltops,
 Where the eyes have a kingdom to roam;
See the scudding clouds scattering glory,
 O'er the fields round our forefathers home.

Ling'ring down by the haven at twilight,
 Sheer and rugged rocks etch the pale sky;
Sounding shill through the surging waves turmoil,
 Breaks a lone scorrie's wandering cry;
Dusky boaties sway lightly at anchor,
 With their lobster pots spread on the quay;
Cadent song of the tumbling river,
 Overwhelmed by the challenging sea.

ALONG THE NORTH COAST

Meeting round a friend's fire after dayset,
Telling Caithness tales ancient and new;
From the sea and the soil comes our birthright,
Down the years rings our heritage through;
With the star-spangled night for our going,
And the gleam in the north for our guide;
We keep faith with our folks gone before us,
And the northland we cherish with pride.

George McLeod.

WIND

The 'plane rose through the murk of an "Auld Reekie" haar into the brightness of the sunshine above the clouds and droned along between silver and blue till we came down at Dyce. Up again through the "blanket" and out over the invisible sea. In due course we turned west, left the haar behind and there was Caithness, with the Pentland Firth and the Orkneys alone in their glory basking in the sunshine of a lovely morning in March. Completely cut off from the south by a wall of mist, they looked as indeed they are, places apart from the rest of the country. The county never looked grander than it did then. The unkind may say that it was the contrast between murk and light, but to my mind, that was not the case. The land looked well, the cliffs as impressive as ever and the sea sparkled in the sunshine. From that height, the natives couldn't be   seen, but it has always been my contention that when the land is well, so are the folks. And so it proved.

After a safe landing, we drove along the familiar road to the "bonniest village" of them all, enjoying the sunshine, getting up to date with the news and congratulating ourselves on the pleasant outlook of a week's settled weather. It was not to be! Unfortunately, during the night an easterly gale had sprung up and from the back door – to me at least – there was a most unusual scene. The waves in Dunnet Bay were all breaking out towards the Firth. Not a wave broke on the sands.

As the storm lasted all that week, there was plenty time to see how the various parts of the county were affected. The most sheltered spot seemed to be Thirsa esplanade – like the rest of the town – deserted. The bay was surprisingly calm, due to the wind blowing the waves flat! At Barrock, the wind "blasted" through the house and one door had to be shut before another could be opened. It reminded me very much of the black-out precautions of a ship. At home, tragedy struck when the wind swept round the clove and blew the papers out of the "grieve's" hand. He caught up with one page of the "Scottish Farmer" half a mile up the road, but the morning papers were never seen again. The

MAGIC OF CAITHNESS

Scottish Farmer was a real loss!

Wick felt the full blast on the "baldest" of God's bays – R. L. Stevenson described it – a mass of foam with heavy seas throwing spray high on to the north head. From the south head, it was an awe inspiring sight. It goes without saying that the harbour was closed to all shipping. Despite all the high winds, one single daffodil was in bloom in the front garden of a house in Wick! The finest I had seen in the north or south and a reminder that gales won't last forever. The spring had arrived in the north. Further south, there were heavy falls of snow, but Caithness retained a weather of her own. Sunshine, rain and wind – above all – wind.

Malcolm MacKenzie.
Edinburgh Caithness Magazine.

PAST MIDNIGHT

Cats curl for sleep – past midnight
   Says the clock.

Furl your mind, fold books away:
   Then as the wind
Sinks, and then rises, close this door:
   Dark's door stands open.

Lights have gone out across the plain.
The moon, with punctual lantern held up high.
   Looks in, unshadowed.

The dawn is not so far.
But this is winter, when, from hour
To cere-cloth hour, the light and darkness mingle.

Patiently sleep the trees
Leafless along their leaning boughs.
Rooted in their own dreams the mountains sleep.

Now silence, like a tale
Filled with strange meanings, stretches everywhere,
Complete, profound – and half the world is gone
A pilgrimage the feet can never follow.

Arthur Ball.

Barrock was the inspiration for this poem. Arthur resided in Barrock from 1970 until his death in 1994. "Past Midnight" was one of his favourite poems.

Arthur Ball – The Barrock Poet.
Photographed by Ronald Thomson.

83

MEMORIES OF ARTHUR BALL

One of the highlights of a recent Caithness holiday was meeting veteran Barrock poet Arthur Ball, and recording some of his Neil Gunn memories.

We were seated above the Trinkie Pool, at Wick, with a grandstand view of the sea, as Arthur reminisced about the Dunbeath novelist and his wife, Daisy.

"I actually met him for the first time in 1933" explained Arthur, retired school-teacher and author of five poetry books. It was an early poem of Arthur Ball's which caught the eye of Neil Gunn in a Wick magazine. The title was "Caithness" and the second verse reads:

> Thy face unpassioned lies,
> Stone to the kindred moon,
> Stone to the sun,
> Kind only to the twilight star,
> When evening's silver moon,
> Shivers away unto the sunset-bar.

Neil wrote an enthusiastic letter to the poet, and also suggested an invitation to join the Scottish Renaissance group.

Arthur Ball declined, as he was largely of English parentage, although born in Wick. He was grateful, however, for Neil's interest, and also for the letter Gunn had written to the John O'Groat Journal about the Caithness poem.

Returning from a holiday in England in 1933, Arthur Ball decided to call at the Gunn's Inverness home in Dochfour Drive. By this time Neil Gunn had written four novels and a book of short stories. Two of the novels are now regarded as classic Gunn books: "Morning Tide" (1931) and "Sun Circle" (1933). Arthur said that over a glass of whisky, the ice was broken, and talk flowed easily. Neil was a customs and excise officer in Inverness, another four years were to pass before he came a full-time writer – that was after "Highland River" (1937).

In 1942, Arthur Ball was stationed at Dingwall with the RASC, and this prompted a visit to the Gunn's, who were then resident at Braefarm House near Dingwall.

"I used to go there on a Sunday and we had many chats. Neil Gunn was such an original, and Mrs Gunn was very charming, a most loveable person", recalled Arthur.

"They had a beautiful sitting room. It was homely with a lovely deep carpet, a sort of creamy colour. Neil would sit in his armchair with his feet on a crimson hassock. I noticed he had signed copies of the Grassic

Gibbon Trilogy, just by his elbow on the bookshelf."

By 1942, Neil Gunn had penned his most famous novel, "The Silver Darlings" (1941) and the core of Caithness books which established his name as a notable Scottish writer.

"He was a down to earth intellectual", said Arthur. "There was no artificiality about Neil Gunn, and he had this sense of humour which was a great saving grace."

Speaking of Daisy Gunn, Arthur said she was the ideal partner for Neil; where he was sometimes brooding and introspective, she was outgoing, and the contrast was perfect. Her philosophy could be summed up in one word – kindness.

From Dingwall, Arthur went to Muir of Ord, and reckoned he visited the Gunns some five or six times between 1942 and '43. On his last visit to Braefarm, the two men took a walk up to the moors which lay above the Gunn's home. Anyone who knows this part of the Highlands will surely agree that the Heights of Brae affords one of the finest views, and it is in this locale that the Neil Gunn Memorial (1987) may be found. The Gunns lived at Braefarm for some 12 years, and in this setting Neil found inspiration for many of his splendid and evocative essays which appeared in "Highland Pack" (1949).

Arthur Ball was posted to GHQ in Hounslow, London, and never met the Gunns again, although he corresponded from time to time and dedicated his 1954 book of poems, "A Place for Tritons" to Neil Gunn.

Was Neil Gunn a genius? "His genius was greater than his talent, if you know what I mean," said Arthur. "He wasn't very good at "pot boiling" in my opinion. He had to be at his best to be good. But when he was at his best, he was superb".

A postscript from Arthur Ball arrived while this article was being completed, "Sun Circle" captivated me from the very first page. It all seemed so effortless – yet so vivid. Those people from long ago moved before me in mystery and magic, yet with feet firmly placed on the ground. They were part and parcel of their setting – surely in the nice Dunbeath Strath – which also came directly alive.

"Smoke from their fire all but curled up from the pages. Unlike some of the violence in certain other of his books, such as "The Lost Glen" and "The Outer Landscape", the violence, when it does occur in "Sun Circle" seems inevitable, as it were foredained. One is perhaps horrified but one isn't repelled or disgusted. It is part of the whole fabric of the story, as is the self-killing of the captive woman of high rank as she is led to the Viking ships."

"I would suggest there is a quality akin to music in this book. It stands apart from the rest of Gunn's work. Though I am not suggesting that "Morning Tide" or "The Silver Darlings" are in any way less fine in their own way. But I am surprised that such a masterpiece as "Sun Circle" was allowed to stay out of print so long – that up to now it has surely not received an iota of the praise it merits."

"I don't know what guided Gunn's writing hand here. There is no so called "poetic prose" in it – yet it is of the gold of true poetry. This is only my opinion, of course, but I feel in this I am not wrong."

One likes to think of Neil Gunn and Arthur Ball as kindred spirits, each in their way – literary craftsmen of a special kind. My thanks to Arthur Ball for his cordial memories of Neil Gunn in this centenary year.

R.T., John O'Groat Journal (1991).

STARLINGS

Thousands wheeling above the stubble-field,
  Over the field and down;
And I, the watching one, less solitary,
  Than Morven, blue and calm, and near today.
The gleaming skeins of starlings,
  Above the gathered field;
From the grey-feathered cloud a black cloud wheeling,
  Exquisite skeins of silence;
If I walk out, clear wing sounds, glittering wings;
  Wordless, yet language perfect;
No loom to weave by, yet this weaving,
  Vanishing suddenly, here for ever.

Arthur Ball.
Valley of Wild Birches.

THE MAGIC OF CAITHNESS

Thirteen miles east-north-east of Thurso stands the hamlet of Mey and at the foot of a woodland drive may be found the Castle of Mey, which is the Queen Mother's holiday home in Caithness. The Castle of Mey – or Barrogill Castle as it used to be known – dates back to the 16th century, and faces the Pentland Firth. It is in fact the only Royal home which faces the sea, and the view north is especially fine on a summer day when the Firth is calm and the sea a magnetic blue.

The Castle of Mey used to be the property of the Earls of Caithness, indeed it was built for George, the fourth Earl of Caithness, between 1566 and 1572. When the Queen Mother first saw the Castle, with her friends Commander and Lady Doris Vyner, in the summer of 1952, it was a rundown place with a neglected walled garden, but the Queen

Mother realised its potential and purchased the estate.
It is said the Queen Mother's love of Caithness began when she stayed as a guest of the Vyners at their Dunnet home, "The House of the Northern Gate [1]"; one can imagine how impressed the Royal visitor would be with the superb view across Dunnet Bay, especially at sunset, for the house is situated atop Dwarwick Head in a commanding position.

It took three years before the Castle of Mey was made habitable again – the autumn of 1955 – and in all some 12 years to restore the castle to prime condition. The end result is said to be very satisfying, preserving the past, yet allowing modern amenities too: for above all it is a home, not a museum.

J.T. CALDER

"As a people, the Caithnessians are acute, shrewd and practical with a decided turn for business", thus wrote James Traill Calder, retired schoolmaster and poet, now remembered as Historian of Caithness.

His History, published in 1861, quickly sold out and became a notable book of its kind. It was based on two main sources: the writings of Thormod Torfeson (Torfeaus) and Sir Robert Gordon's "Genealogical History of the Earldom of Sutherland".

Calder also gleaned data from books, letters and family records. His research cost a great deal of effort yet he considered the project a labour of love. One criticism of Calder's History, was the amount of barbarism recorded. Calder conceded this, but added, Caithness was no more violent in the past, than the rest of Scotland.

In the latter part of the book, Calder refers to the lowly state of country schoolmasters. As an ill-paid dominie, he spoke from experience – his retiral pension was a mere 25 pounds per annum.

Calder held a high opinion of his fellow Caithnessians: "The men are hardy, active and well made, and the women are in general exceedingly good looking."

Calder modestly described his history as a "sketch or outline" yet it has proved to be an invaluable work which has not been superseded. Those who wish to learn of the civil and traditional "History of Caithness" from the 10th century should seek out an edition of "Calder".

Historians like Calder [2] seek out from musty tomes and dry legal documents, something of our heritage. Wars and rumours of Wars mar

[1] *Originally known as Dwarwick House, built for Vice Admiral Sir E. S. Alexander Sinclair, KCB. MVO.*

[2] *The memorial statue to historian Calder may be seen on the south bank of Wick Riverside. It was erected in July 1900.*

the record, yet perhaps the balance may show faltering steps toward civilisation and the hopes of a peaceful future?

"Historian of Caithness", Wick Riverside.
Photographed: Ronald Thomson.

The secretary of the Glasgow Literary Society, John Mowat, kept note of the Calder Memorial in his scrapbook. In early 1899 a Memorial Committee was organised, and Caithness exiles invited to subscribe.

By April 1900, the organisers were sufficiently assured of obtaining the money that they ordered a seven foot high marble statue through John Horne as agent for sculptors in Carrera, Italy.

"The monument was fashioned from a model of Calder made by John Nicolson of Nybster, who composed it from portraits – taking the forehead from one, the nose from another, the mouth and chin from a third. . ." The end result was said to be realistic.

CHAPTER 5
A BOYAG'S WONDERLAND

A DYKESIDE ECSTASY

"This is perfect!"

I addressed myself: involuntarily expressing my sense of gratitude and delight.

I had just sat down on the inner side of a warm, towsy ditch; my back to a venerable dyke, and my face to the sun.

The sky was mottled after the prevailing style of skies in Cattiland. Grey pewter-coloured clouds were anchored near the earth and these were topped by voluminous cumulus formations which thinned up to transparency and vanished in vast lagoons of ravishing blue. The sun was happy in his power behind them, leaping through at every gap with a sudden flare that seemed a gesture of merriment. A cooling, fawning wind tempered the atmosphere and made glad every nerve. Far before me the heather galloped for lingering miles. I saw no living thing save a derelict sea-gull and a wandered curlew – types of the monastic exclusion of the hills.

"This is perfect!" I repeated, congratulating myself.

What converging circumstances created so much satisfaction? Could I analyse them?

Of course, I was a townsman, albeit with a countryman's temperament. And here was I, released from the monotonous infelicities of streets and offices, and planted once more amid the frank and planless scenes of my affection! Even men who never think of green fields or russet hills all the year round are thrilled by an unwonted pleasure when holiday-time delivers them to the experience. The contrast is so amazing! For an interval, there is no labour, no responsibility – only the exuberance of freedom; no clock to consider or timetables to study – only a vast relief that somehow seems divine! Is it any wonder, then, that one who dreams of hills and moorlands 12 months in the year should gulp at the chance of release, like a hungry boy at a plate of rare temptation? I was in an imperial mood, and felt no envy even of angels! And the day was faultless, one of those days "that scarce dare breathe, they are so beautiful", as some poet sings. Every wish was gratified: not even curiosity remained.

I can imagine no engrossment so flattering to one's capacity for happiness as that of sitting thus beside an old grey wall on a sunny day. To drop gradually all control of your sense-faculties and let the mind drift; to anchor your eyes on some swatch of blue till you fancy the stars are coming through; to hear the lark as if you were in a trance, the sounds quivering as those of some cherub from happier times; to be quiescent to everything save the welcome, inexpressible happiness of it all – this, I am sure, makes cheap even an opium dream.

Of course, this indulgence may seed in sentimentalism. The sentimentalist is content with his reverie, and he gluts himself with it; but it entices him no further. He sings –

"Dearest mood of all the year!
Aimless, idle and content –
Sky, and wave, and atmosphere
Wholly indolent!"

The genuine rapture, however, is a tonic, not a drug; an inspiration, not an opiate; and it afterwards translates itself into terms of life and affection. Who sees Cattiland thus will prove his attachment by deeds of loyalty. "We must act our dreams, not dreams, our acts."

Commonplace wild flowers were within reach of my hand. Buttercups, hyacinths, ragged robin, perky cloverheads, and tussocks of bog myrtle waited my appreciation. Nature's gentle ministries – so medicinal to fatigued spirits! "Consider the lilies of the field" (not of the hothouse) said the greatest Naturalist Teacher. And why? "They toil not, neither do they spin." Labour, strife, anxiety – these contribute no impulse to their sweet and beautiful existence. The secret is Repose and Humility: and no life can be serene without these.

Are you familiar with the perfume of the bog-myrtle? I do not know any wild flower that is so suggestive of Nature's unaided attempt to be at once wholesome and refined. It is pungent, and of the earth; but vernal and dainty. The Arabs have a legend that when Adam was expelled from Paradise he was permitted to take three things with him – a handful of wheat, for food; some dates, as fruit; and a sprig of myrtle, to perfume the world. So the myrtle is a souvenir of lost Eden!

The bog myrtle is as ancient as the hills on which it grows; it has an unpretentious rusticity and self-content which gives instant pleasure; and its fragrance is distinct and penetrating. And are not these some of the characteristics of the people of Cattiland, and of Cattiland itself?

Let us adopt it as our emblem! The bour-tree may be more in evidence, but you cannot fondle a tree. Besides, the myrtle is in every way daintier.

I was resting against a hoary dyke – a real Cattiland specimen. It was built chiefly of stones taken off the land and set to their task all undressed, with occasional through-stones for strength and equilibrium, and a coping of turf.

Reared of dry stones! This is an art that goes back to the very beginning of things – the earliest craft of all, most likely. The dyke outwears all fences of wood and iron many times, shelters your sheep and cattle, defines your rights indisputably, and gathers a fund of sentiment as it ages.

All the stones were grey, and lichen had pinned many medals on them for their brave persistence. Scraggy stalks of grass groped their way through the gaps and attempted to plug them, but the wind was scarcely hindered. How long it had stood, I cannot say, nor the generations of man and beast it had sheltered; but it was weather-hacked and weary looking. All Cattilanders know such dykes – worn serfs that guard the garden of their father's "hoosie", skirt the kirk and school, and detail the croftships of their boyhood's district. Every native who retains the home instinct in his blood recognises them with a gush of old-world affection. As I sat there, the wind searched through the interspaces and whispered to me many unrecordable memories and suggestions. And each leal heart can guess them!

"Too sombre for me", sighs the globe-trotter. "I look for some spice and kick in my holiday." Certainly; but, gentle sir, have you never observed that all perfect pleasures are serious? When children begin to dance they are chatty and noisy; but as the dance floats into order and rhythm their spirits quieten, and they only laugh again when it is completed. Great music smothers flippancy. The higher the peak the deeper the silence. Tense love is always serious. It may begin in pleasantries; but as the passion tightens, its objects become earnest and grave.

Whatever is perfect is serious, "too deep for sound or foam".

John Horne – Summer Days in Cattiland (1929).

A BOYAG'S WONDERLAND

The wide and sundrenched moorland scene
    Lies outspread far before the cottage door,
Revealing to a boyag's eager gaze
    A wonderland of sight and sound, all beckoning
To rich adventure.
    To wander forth among its mysteries
Absorbing all its native majesty
    In undisturbed communion.
Some chord of hidden heritage is touched
    That links so many generations gone before
With youth's awakening.
    And so reclined upon a favoured wayside bank
A well-cropped couch of tangled grass and tiny heather
    Basking in warmth.
A myriad maze of mossy plants and flowerets – many hued
    Drowses the perfumed air with scents
Distilled in fairyland.
    This wonder-world of lone day-dreaming drifts along
Like ever-changing clouds from Morven's heights,
    Trailing weird shadows over dale and hill
To vanish in oblivion beyond the sight,
    somewhere unseen.
The drumming snipe repeats his antic flight,
    The whaup and tumbling schochad's eerie cries,
And elsewhere too, an ambling cart is heard
    Returning home along some rugged heather track.
Amidst the tufted rushes lies the flagstone well
    Where clink of pail and pitcher sounds in harmony
With simple Caithness life.
    At nightfall when the hammal peat-reek spreads
Its fragrant spell
    The ghostly, awesome tulloch hill recedes from view,
Leaving the Will-O-Wisp to shed its magic light
    In phantom mystery.

George McLeod.

There are Caithness roads which take the traveller to remote
landscapes where distance is paramount. The sense of isolation is
heightened by the flatness of the countryside, and vast tracts of
moorland scenery – now titled "The Flow Country".
    Because of its featureless landscape, Caithness can look bleak and

daunting in inclement weather, but when the sun shines then the coin is reversed, for Caithness has a potent beauty under the northern light.

Seasoned travel writer, T. Ratcliffe, Barnett, reflected the magic of Caithness this way: "Some people will tell you that there is no beauty about the Caithness flats. But there is a beauty that is all its own about flat countries – long swathes of greens and blues and yellows and browns, which can only be seen where the distances are limitless.

The Caithness skies are as wide, as splendid as those of Holland, and we know how the great Dutch painters loved to paint them.

Wherever you go along this road by the Pentland seas you will also see the perfect poem in gold and blue – the long line of yellow cornfields meeting the sapphire seas. And for the light! Dawns and sunsets are never so beautiful as when they are seen over a wide or level land."

In a BBC Radio broadcast, Neil Gunn remarked how unforgettable were the summer mornings of his childhood, watching the fishing boats coming home – well the herring days have long since gone – but the summer mornings can be fascinating as ever.

One recalls a superb morning at Scarfskerry, (close by an azure sea) having breakfast out of doors, there was a novelty in the experience, which made it the highlight of our holiday at Greengoe Croft.

Those from warmer climes may take their weather for granted, and eating outside as normal, but in our northern zone, breakfast outside was as surprising as it was welcome.

The unexpected makes a Caithness holiday more memorable and something of a red-letter day, hence our delightful incident at Scarfskerry in the month of June.

THE GLAMOUR OF OUR MOORLANDS

Our beloved Caithness is endowed with a wealth of natural features that throughout the centuries has moulded the character and psychology of her people, and presented a marvellous variety of entrancing aspects that reveal the glory of nature's abundant beauty.

The solitary mountain majesty of Morven presides over a wide range of remote hills, framing an impressive bulwark against the southern sky, while other scattered ranges dominate the western horizons most effectively, leaving the remaining boundaries of the county as ramparts against the incessant onslaught of the ocean upon our shores.

Enclosed within these confines repose the manifold diversities that ever inspire the natives, and fascinate our visitors in all seasons of the year. A rambling survey can locate our heaths and hillags, straths and dales, lochs and tarns, while around the coasts prevail the cliffs and cletts, harbours and beaches, rugged roads and geos, rivers and chattering burnies fringing the restless seas that rage or croon in endless moods.

Beside the verdant farmlands stand isolated woodlands and coppices, prominent among the crofts and rodies that pattern the countryside, and in their close precincts a wariness exists that can startle with the sudden scuffling of a bird among the dead leaves.

In the dense forests, the instinctive fear of hidden dangers can be most pronounced in the trackless depths, and return to open skies a welcome relief, all tension deported.

A most entrancing experience rewards the cliff-top rambler who finds a sheltered cranny, from whence plunging seas, vagrant ships, and the rugged grandeur of a craggy coastline, that is the perpetual haunt of clamorous birdlife, can all be comprehensively enjoyed within the passing hour with all its changing aspects. Many of us have achieved the thrilling moment when we breasted the last few steps to stand supreme upon a mountain summit, and gaze in ecstasy over the magnificient spectacle with the whole panorama outspread around us, all the obstacles and tribulations of the arduous ascent quite suppressed in the glory of achievement.

But one cannot remain for long on a mountain top, and soon all the anxieties of a difficult descent have to be contemplated and regretfully accomplished.

A final survey of the interior regions confirms the deep conviction that in the widespread kingdom of these isolated moorlands lies the source of our most profound emotions, for there the very frontiers of our northern civilisation were established by the ancient pioneers, whose primitive habitations mark the limit of penetration, with all their effort and endurance in the fierce struggle for existence, leaving the untamed hinterlands to retain their inscrutible identity inviolate – unconquered.

It is an entrancing experience to recline in solitude upon a heather couch for a few hours, and silently absorb all the influences that flow from the open countenance of the sun-drenched moorlands, and discover that apprehensions gradually fade away, until an amazing sense of security, and affinity with every aspect of time and space, pervades the mind with utter serenity, as though the rich curtains veiling nature's holy of holies have quietly been drawn aside, and a spiritual communion beyond earth's workaday existence bountifully revealed.

Enveloped by this aura of elation, how appropriate it then is, to arise and stride out along the winding, naked road, into the sunset sky, treading the route of an ancient trackway that witnessed the nomad travellings throughout the ages, when solitary standing stones guided the way in times of blinding mists, or smothering snows, and merely to lay a reverent hand upon one of them, signifies a fraternity with our obscure ancestors whose stone circles and ravaged tumuli among the heatherlands, disclose ample evidence of their primitive history over generations that span the centuries of time.

As mile after mile is traversed, the seemingly monotonous spaces reveal a most remarkable variety of colour and contour under the sunset hues, that illuminate the scene in awesome splendour.

Here it is then, that we halt, and pay our profound tribute and homage under this benign benediction, to those long vanished, whose powerful influence remains among the sounds and silences of the vacant moorlands where we can so naturally re-picture their activities and aspirations that still inspire us, and thus elated, we slowly retrace our footsteps, leaving the evening glow to steadily traverse the northern sky and flush into the pearly dawn of another day with all our mundane affairs, but enriched by the stimulus of the celestial glamour of our entrancing moorlands.

George McLeod.
Edinburgh Caithness Magazine.

SEA SHELL

Far from dashing seas
　And windswept shore,
The little shell resides
　Timeless as the moon,
Potent with sunlit memories
　That cross the inward eye.

A seagull soaring above
　The morning tide,
Sea pinks drawing the eye
　To their summer exhibition,
Footprints on wet sand
　Symbols of another beachcomber.

Far from dashing seas
　And windswept shore,
The little white shell
　Whispers in my ear,
And in the silent night
　Echoes the rolling tide.

Ronald Thomson.

Photographed by Dan Mackay.

"Balavreed" – Caithness Remnant.

Ham harbour has long been a ruin, its glory vanquished by stormy seas. Even when we lived in Caithness – 1957-1960 – the little harbour (built by James Bremner) was but a remnant. Yet there was still something to marvel in the great stone slabs, placed together like a giant jigsaw puzzle, a credit to Victorian industry.

From our Corsback, Dunnet, home we made occasional visits to this neuk of Caithness, in search of sea-shells. A treasure trove indeed – for there were countless shells at Ham. The shells were reminiscent of other things: a child's top for example, or another with distinct stripes of brown and orange, like a football strip. Interesting also were shells with a natural sheen, as though a clear varnish has been applied to them. Even the limpet shell, dull at first glance, had underneath, a delicate green colouring.

The surprising discovery of a "Groatie Buckie" shell at Ham was a welcome find. One relates the "Buckie" to the John O'Groats district for that's where they are usually found. Incidentally, necklaces of "Groatie Buckies" are no new ornaments, for the craft dates back some 6,000 years.

One mustn't forget Dunnet Sands where the pièce de résistance was a shell of delicate wafer-thinness like the wings of a butterfly – in miniature. Pink or white, they were elusive, but well worth the effort in finding them.

The beauty of shells is in their individuality; in size, colouring and design. It is intriguing also to speculate where some rare shell may have come from, for the sea is often a restless spirit.

THROUGH THE CAITHNESS LOOKING GLASS
(A short story inspired by the Works of Lewis Carroll)

You may have wondered what became of Alice of Wonderland fame: rumour has it that Alice was seen one sunny morning in Dunnet.

She spotted a bright-eyed cat on a garden wall. "Why, it's my old friend the Cheshire Cat – I'd know that grin anywhere!" "Did you know", said the purring cat, "there are many of your friends here?" "Who?", asked Alice. The Cat stretched and pointed to Dunnet Head. "The King and Queen of Hearts have built a massive castle, but the King is a foolish man." The Cat described how the King had been writing his autobiography out of doors, when a great Caithness wind blew all the papers over the ramparts and as far away as Wick. The King offered a reward for his manuscript. "Unfortunately", added the Cat, "Tweedledum and Tweedledee arrived and started a paper chase with the King's paper. The outcome I know not nor care – I'll settle for a saucer of milk in preference to a stuffy book." And with that the Cat vanished over the wall.

Meanwhile, Dunnet beach was deserted except for the Carpenter and the Walrus. The Carpenter was looking at footprints in the sand. "Ah!, those are a child's prints, and you'll never guess whose!" The Walrus gave a shrug. "Well, it was little Alice in Wonderland. She was paddling here an hour ago – you were snoring at the time." "Such a charming child", said the Walrus, "I must compose a song in her honour – and you will be the first to hear it."

"You may have wondered what brought the child so far from home", said the Carpenter with an air of authority, "well, Alice had read all about John O'Groats and his house, so she decided she would like his autograph." The Walrus stroked his whiskers and looked thoughtful.

But let us now return to Alice who had found some of the King's notepaper. She followed the trail and found herself at a shabby derelict country railway station. As she peered in the waiting room, an eccentric figure with a tall grey hat ran along the platform blowing a whistle and waving a tattered green flag. She recognised it as the Mad Hatter. "All tickets please", he shouted, "I hear a train in the distance", and with that, grabbed the astonished Alice by the hand, ran up some steps, crossed the bridge and arrived on the opposite platform. "Why did we do that?" asked Alice. "Because it's the done thing", sniffed the Hatter, whipping out a yellow-faced watch. " The trains are always late – I don't understand it", he sighed. Alice laughed. "No wonder, this station's been closed for 10 years." "Prove it", said the Hatter looking annoyed and disbelieving. They recrossed the bridge and Alice pointed to the notice in the waiting room. "That explains such a lot", said the Hatter peering at Alice. "I remember you now – you were the girl who came to my tea party years ago and asked all sorts of funny questions." "Yes", said Alice, "and you gave such funny answers". They both laughed. "Speaking of tea parties – let's have another. We'll look for the Dormouse and the cheeky White Rabbit." "That sounds fun", said Alice.

"Climb on the back of my tandem", said the Hatter, "and we'll travel the country in style."

Off they went, a rather curious sight. It was summer and they burst into song as they pedalled.

Tweedledum and Tweedledee, those fat schoolboys, had almost put the King's manuscript together after scouring Caithness for months in all weathers. "Five more pages and the reward is ours", they agreed.

At that moment Alice and the Hatter arrived on the tandem at the Post Office and Alice went in to buy some stamps. Tweedledum and Tweedledee had noticed Alice had some of the King's notepaper sticking out from her shoulder-bag. They waited till she left the post office, then snatched the pages of manuscript from her bag and took to their heels.

A BOYAG'S WONDERLAND

"Oh", shouted Alice, "Those awful boys. They must be stopped. If only there was a policeman". The excitement was too much for the Hatter and he fainted. As Alice knew about first aid, he soon recovered. From the shop next to the post office came the March Hare and the White Rabbit who seemed to be having an argument as to who could run the faster. "The way to settle the matter", said the Mad Hatter, "is to have a race – I'll be judge. Now, White Rabbit, you and Alice use my tandem and see if you can catch Hare". So the Hatter blew his railway whistle, and Alice hung on as the tandem sped down the long road. The March Hare being clever, cut across the fields like lightning.

Eventually, Alice and the White Rabbit passed Tweedledum and Tweedledee on the road and Alice was able to snatch the manuscript from Tweedledum's hand. On the case went – passed Quintfall and Keiss, then through the Moorland Road till they reached John O'Groats. Alice was interested to learn the history of Groats.

As to who had won the race: it was obviously the March Hare, and so the victor was duly toasted.

"Now", said Alice, "it's time to visit the King and give him the missing pages of his book". So Alice and her companions – the Mad Hatter, Dormouse, March Hare and White Rabbit set off through the moors of talking flowers. "Did you know", said the little Dormouse, "that the King and Queen have brought their animated cards with them?"

The road narrowed as they approached the castle. As they came to the King's ornate coach, the Queen of Hearts was shouting at the King, "Don't just sit there – do something". The King poked his head out of the window and shouted back more nonsense. Alice strode up to the royal coach and asked, "Where are your servants?" The Queen of Hearts waved her fan wearily and explained they were either inside the castle watching the World Cup on television, or had left. Alice ordered everyone out of the coach – and out came Humpty Dumpty, the Cheshire Cat, grinning as ever; the White Knight, the Red Knight, Tweedledee and Tweedledum, all looking just as Tenniel had drawn them. The White Rabbit took the driver's seat while the Hatter gave the horses some carrots. The others gave the coach a push – and then – it was "Home James!" for the castle.

Soon the trumpets sounded a fanfare from the ramparts. Alice danced for the royal party, and everyone took to the floor for a "Dashing White Sergeant". The meal was a splendid affair. Later fireworks lit up the dusky northern sky. . . and there Alice in Wonderland's notes stopped as her pen had run dry!

Alan Thomson.
Edinburgh Caithness Magazine, 1983.

DUNNET SANDS

Restless wind, cloudy sky,
  Pale sand, sea-girt rocks,
In a pool of water
Ripples appear like thoughts,
  In the questing mind;
A bird descends, effortless,
And takes refreshment
  With a graceful air;
Neath high stacked dunes
  A trio of children
Telegraph their joy,
  Fragments of sand-castles
Reflect life's transient scene;
  Two birds wing west
In search of Shangri La,
  Pieces of Caithness jigsaw
Found by the mystic sea.

Ronald Thomson. – To Mary and George Gunn, Caithness.

When I turned in to the famous sands of Dunnet, on the Pentland Firth, a solitary caravan from England was the only sign of the holiday spirit along that golden shore. It seemed like a prodigious waste of nature's kindness, for the sun was shining, and turquoise waves, like mile-long furrows curling smoothly from the mould board of a giant plough, followed each other across the sands to break in shallow rushes of froth.

I had not gone there, however, to admire the sands of Dunnet. I was more interested in the village, for it is linked with the name of Timothy Pont, the first Scottish map-maker. It is sad to reflect that his name and his great achievement mean so little to modern Scots, for there is not the slightest doubt that he is our unknown and unhonoured genius – and this is a country dotted with grandiose monuments to titled men who never accomplished anything.

Timothy Pont became minister at Dunnet in 1601. He was the second son of the Rev. Robert Pont, minister of St. Cuthbert's, Edinburgh, and distinguished himself as a mathematician at the University of St. Andrew. The Ponts were important people in church circles, the elder Pont having been offered the Bishopric of Caithness, which he declined. Timothy's elder brother Zachary, whose father-in-law was the formidable John Knox, was minister of the Caithness parish of Bower. It seems almost certain, therefore, that Timothy accepted the pastorship at Dunnet in order to have the time to make his famous survey.

In any case, he proceeded to collect data for an Atlas of Scotland, and he completed it, although he did not live to see it published. His manuscripts were left in the hands of relatives, who did not realise how valuable they were. So they lay around, gathering damp and being eaten by mice and moths, until they were in real danger of being damaged beyond repair. Eventually, however, they passed into the hands of John Blaeu of Amsterdam, and appeared in the great atlas he published in 1668. The publication of Pont's maps in that atlas identified him as the first and greatest cartographer that Scotland had produced.

John Herries McCulloch.
The Charm of Scotland.

Dunnet Head! The very name strikes a familiar note from our Corsback days when my twin brother Alan and I made our first visit one January day.

John O'Groats we knew from boyhood days at Will Reid's Quintfall Farm at Lyth – but the attraction of Dunnet Head was to visit the most northern point on the Scottish mainland, no doubt about that!

Anticipation was the keynote as we drove the long winding road in an old Hillman car which had seen better days; the ascending moorland route, interspersed with Lochans, seemed like a little world on its own – yet the sense of isolation was part of its appeal and a fitting preface toward the lighthouse terminal.

Who could fail to be impressed with the view from Dunnet Head? In a flat county like Caithness, the contrast is greater for its elevation; a grandstand view of the sea, with the frontier of Orkney framing the horizon.

Countless seas have crashed against the cliffs at Dunnet Head since we made our debut visit in 1958, but the attraction of this northern outpost has never dimmed nor its charm lessened.

At one time Dunnet Head Lighthouse (erected in 1831) was the highest in Scotland; 346 feet above high water and a visit to its tower a notable experience.

John Horne has written: "The vast prairie of the North Sea rolls boundless beyond, carrying the thoughts to the Far Away; and the Orkney Islands dot the magnificent surface like blobs of paint on a sheet of glass." (County of Caithness 1907.)

Regarding Dunnet Head, two names come to mind – Willie Dunnet and Johnnie Sinclair, distinctive characters in their own right. It was Will Dunnet, our Corsback neighbour, who taught Alan and I how to cut peat up on Dunnet Head, and it was John Sinclair who found a buyer for my vintage car: a lighthouse keeper bought it for £30 in 1960!

Willie Dunnet had the distinction of being the oldest precentor in the Church of Scotland and on June 3, 1959, in the Britannia Hall, Dunnet, a presentation was made to celebrate his leading congregational singing for over 60 years.

Willie was in his 80s when he showed us peat cutting, and had great faith in the medicinal qualities of Dunnet Head – he claimed the pure air cleared him of tuberculosis. A mixture of moor and sea makes the air royal on Dunnet Head.

Johnnie Sinclair, ex-merchant seaman, deserved a place in the Caithness hall of memory: for 40 years, via his school taxi service, he conveyed children from Dunnet Head to Crossroads School, along a road which between the wars was "little better than a cart track with deep ruts and foot deep potholes."

The single track to the lighthouse in deep snow was no easy matter, even for someone like Johnnie, yet in 40 years through all kinds of weather he never had one accident.

The spare-framed figure, familiar in beret, was a self-taught driver, an expert mechanic and an authority on vintage cars. I recall seeing him driving up the steep brae from Brough Pier in a large robust looking pre-war car, and he acknowledged me with a wave.

Alan and Ronald Thomson at Corsback, Dunnet, in 1958.
Photographed by Gordon Thomson.

Local people gifted him a wallet of notes on his retirement, plus a beautiful barometer in a ship's wheel design; while the "Groat" paid tribute to this Caithness worthie via an illustrated article.

Travel writer Gwen Moffat has written of how she came north one hot afternoon to investigate Duncansby Head for the first time, and how she later drove round to Dunnet Head, spending the night beside a lochan.

Like many a traveller in Caithness, she discovered something enchanting: "Caithness is a place, only partly land, that slips into no slot. There is no Gaelic; the names are Norse and curiously familiar but it is a county steeped in ancient history and unbelievably strange. It is wild and magical and tempting with a spell cast, not by people, or even by fairies, but by the elements." (Sunday Telegraph 1974).

To have seen Dunnet Head from the land is one thing, and to have seen it from the sea another. I recall Alan telling me how he saw Dunnet Head from the cruise ship Uganda in 1976; it was a welcome sight of home after visiting Germany, Denmark and Norway.

I once saw the towering cliff scenery of Dunnet Head from the St. Ola during an evening cruise; interesting indeed to experience this special landmark from a different perspective.

It is intriguing to read in Calder's History of Caithness that Dunnet Head may be the Cape Orcase of Sicilian Diororus (BC 53), the first reference to any part of Scotland.

Speaking of geographical pioneers, it was Timothy Pont, minister of Dunnet from 1601-1610, who drew up the first maps of Scotland.

It seems surprising that there is nothing to inform tourists to Dunnet Head that they have reached the most northern part of mainland Scotland. I recall two young German tourists last September who were unaware of this. One thought Cape Wrath northernmost – understandable, albeit incorrect.

After the request that I, "make a picture", they posed on an outlying piece of cliff without, it seemed, any fear of danger! Cautioning them to be careful, I quickly took their photograph with my zoom lens, while the evening sun cast its own epitaph.

Over the years, Alan and I have made many holiday movies in Caithness. Being twins, we shared similar interests, including cine photography and still photography. In 1982 we made "Summer Days in Caithness" with our stepfather, Lyndesay G. Langwill, location work included Forss Falls, Thurso Beach and Riverside, Lybster, Wick, and of course, Dunnet Head.

Perhaps the highlight of this filmic tour for Lyndesay, was an excursion to Forsinard Station in Sutherland, as our stepfather was a railway buff from the days of steam. There is great potential for the

MAGIC OF CAITHNESS

film-maker in Caithness, and it would be nice if Grampian Television might consider a Caithness documentary sometime – they did a fine job with their Wick quater-centenary tribute. "No Mean Town" (1989).

In the six-volume collection The Scots Minstrelsy there is a Caithness song titled "Keen Blaws the Wind Ower Donocht Head" which impressed Robert Burns to write: "Donocht Head is not mine. I would give 10 pounds it were."

One may only speculate what impression Dunnet Head might have had on our national poet had he visited Caithness during his Highland Tour, but it is fair to suggest the stark grandeur and commanding height might have inspired a poem at least.

To stand atop Dunnet Head on a still summer night, with the setting sun glowing across the vast expanse of sea, is to experience not only the magic of Caithness but also a strong sense of peace.

May this special place remain unspoilt, holding fast its secrets, yet inspiring new impressions with each dawn.

R.T., John O'Groat Journal.

CAITHNESS

Where are steep cliffs, deep caves, and seas
    That rage and smile?
Come! Follow me where are few trees,
    Let us beguile
The hours by singing with the breeze
    In Caithness.

Love you wild flowers and scents, and bright
    And golden days;
Snow in the winter crisp and white;
    Old hymns of praise?
Come with me then, my dear, to-night
    To Caithness.

Know now a county bleak and bare
    With blooming heather,
Cheerless and cold it looks, yet fair
    To us. Together,
We have explored it. And how rare
    Is Caithness!

Alexander Miller.

WILD SEA

Wild sea o'er the rocks
  More potent than words
Dashing o'er the harbour wall
  With careless abandon
White as the gannet's breast.

Wild sea swift and relentless
  Casting away dreams
Into the vortex of night
  Primeval picture unbridled
With cymbals crashing triumphant!

> *Ronald Thomson*
> *To my brother Gordon.*
> *Edinburgh Caithness Magazine.*

THE MAGIC OF CAITHNESS

The splendour of an August sky
  Gilding the Pentland Firth
Casting away idle dreams
  Into a superb reality.

The quiet precinct of Mey
  Touching the hem of time
Blending picturesque images
  Of Caithness in her prime.

The afterglow on castle windows
  Drawing the eye like a magnet
The scent of myriad flowers
  Potent as the evening sun.

Snow white gulls echoing cry
  Across the lonely shore
The first star of night
  Touching the soul anew.

> *Ronald Thomson*
> *Dedicated to Queen Elizabeth, the Queen Mother at the time of her 90th*
> *birthday and in memory of her long and happy association with*
> *Caithness, via her Castle of Mey holiday home.*

"Gutting a catch on board a Wick seine-netter".

Photographed by Dan Mackay.

CAITHNESS FLAGSTONES

These are the way they trod
Upon these warm and polished flagstones
Hewn from the earth's face
In this our cherished land.

And still we hear
The tread of heavy boots
The swish of oilskins in the rain
The music of Gaelic songs,
From the open windows
We saw not the singers.

And here now they sleep
Still as one with us
In this great universe
Though more content than we
Who still tread
These polished flagstones.

Isabel Richardson.

In 1948, an engraved sundial of Caithness flagstone was ready for erection on a site at Balmoral Castle – this was a wedding gift to Princess Elizabeth, from the county of Caithness.

Castletown came about as a result of the Flagstone Trade, originated by Sheriff James Traill (1758-1843). It was Traill who utilised a natural resource which had been known to prehistoric man in Caithness, thus began an industry which lasted for the best part of a century. The first shipment of flagstone was from Castlehill harbour in 1825. The quarry was only a short distance from the harbour, likewise the cutting yard.

Sheriff Traill lived in Castlehill House, which overlooked the harbour and included a fine view of Dunnet Bay. He was really on home ground, being born in Dunnet Manse on 2nd June, 1758. His father the Rev. George Traill, D.D., an Orcadian, was parish minister at Dunnet.

Sheriff Traill's estate reflected a man of wealth and position: educated at Marischal College, Aberdeen, he studied law in Edinburgh, became an advocate in 1779, then in 1788, Sheriff-Depute of the County of Caithness. Married to Lady Janet Sinclair, a daughter of the Earl of Caithness, he purchased property from the Sinclair family.

Historian Calder says, when Sheriff Traill became proprietor of Castlehill House, there was not a single tree on the estate! Happily, he engaged a forester and started planting trees uncommon to Caithness such as larch, elm and oak, thus the policies were transformed. Traill was a pioneer regarding agricultural improvement in Caithness, and this stands to his credit.

The Flagstone industry was important to Caithness, it gave employment to local men, established Castletown as a village, and its very durable product was used at home and abroad. Tests proved that Caithness flagstone was second to none.

The name "Castletown" might confuse the visitor new to Caithness – for there has never been a castle or town in the vicinity. The village, however, is one of the best known in the county sited on the main Thurso to John O'Groats route.

Robert Louis Stevenson refers to Castletown in his memorable essay: Random Memories: The education of an Engineer.

"We had been upon the road all evening; the coach-top was crowded with Lewis fishers going home, scarce anything but Gaelic had sounded in my ears; and our way had lain over a moorish country very northern to behold. Latish at night, though it was still broad day in our subarctic latitude, we came down upon the shores of the roaring Pentland Firth, that grave of mariners; on one hand, the cliffs of Dunnet Head ran seaward; in front was the little bare, white town of Castletown, its streets full of blowing sand; nothing beyond, but the North Islands, the great deep, and the perennial ice-fields of the Pole. And here, in the last imaginable place, there sprang up young outlandish voices and a chatter of some foreign speech; and I saw, pursuing the coach with its load of Hebridean fishers – as they pursued vetturini up the passes of the Apennines or perhaps along the grotto under Virgil's tomb – two little dark-eyed, white-tooth Italian vagabonds, of 12 to 14 years of age, one with a hurdy-gurdy, the other with a cage of white mice. The coach passed on, and their small Italian chatter died in the distance; and I was left to marvel how they had wandered into that country, and how they fared in it, and what they had thought of it, and when (if ever) they should see again the silver wind-breaks run among the olives, and the stone-pine stand guard upon Etruscan sepulchres.

Upon any American, the strangeness of this incident is somewhat lost. For as far back as he goes in his own land, he will find some alien camping there; the Cornish miner, the French or Mexican half-blood, the negro in the south, these are deep in the woods and far among the mountains. But in an old, cold and rugged country such as mine, the days of immigration are long at an end; and away up there which was at that time far beyond the northernmost extreme of railways, hard upon the shore of that ill-omened strait of whirlpools, in a land of moors

Queen Mother, Commander and Lady Doris Vyner, outside Castle of Mey.
Photographed by John Adams.

where no stranger came unless it should be a sportsman to shoot grouse or an antiquary to decipher runes, the presence of these small pedestrians struck the mind as though a bird-of-paradise had risen from the heather or an albatross come fishing in the bay of Wick."

Caithness used to be well known for its characters, and Castletown, may claim the late Abrach Mackay as one. Many will recall his kenspeckled figure and cheery wave to passers-by. On the 28th February, 1969, the "Groat" reported that Councillor John Abrach Mackay was 94 years old that day and was the "oldest acting Councillor in Scotland and probably in the United Kingdom".

The report included an anecdote about Abrach rounding Cape Horn in one of his brother-in-law's ships during a storm – when huge waves were breaking over the masts.

"He decided to go down to the cabin which he did holding a copy of the John O'Groat Journal in one hand and a small bottle of J. Dewar's whisky in the other hand. After enjoying a good hot toddy, he fell asleep and was wakened well up on the west coast of South America.

On the way from Vancouver to Montreal, he stopped at Glencoe, where he spoke at a meeting of Gaelic and English speaking descendants of Mackays evicted from Strathnaver during the Clearances. He told his audience that no one should ever go round Cape Horn without a drop of Dewar's whisky in his possession. On reaching home two weeks later he found a parcel with a nice present of J. Dewar's whisky awaiting him without the donor's name."

Over the years, Abrach travelled through many lands, including China, Japan, Australia and New Zealand. Abrach's family hailed from Sutherland, and Caithness was home from 1884 – first to Folly Farm, Murkle and a decade later to Castletown.

Abrach was principal of a Civil Service and Business College in Dundee, and in 1914 he went to Canada where he opened a similar college in Montreal.

His name came to the fore as county councillor, and he held his view on all subjects. He opposed the building of the harbour on Stroma, as being too late to halt depopulation, his opposition proved correct, but the harbour was built. Without doubt, Abrach, as he was popularly known, was a Caithness character, a colourful, sometimes controversial, figure on the local scene.

CHAPTER 6
THURSO AND BEYOND

"Change here for Thirsa" – the old familiar cry at Georgemas Junction. For Caithness exiles it was the home stretch, be they from Thurso or Wick. Back to "Kaitness" once more!

In the old days the journey from Inverness was a long slow haul: 39 stations were involved and some six hours of travel. Preface that with six from Edinburgh, plus waiting time at Inverness, and you could write off a whole day.

The Highland Line was very much a social service for rural Scotland – each little station part of the great network. Those were the days when "Steam" was King and rail travel taken for granted.

The coming of the railway to Caithness is a chapter in itself and great must have been the excitement in 1874, when the first train arrived at Wick; what bright horizons it must have conjured up for the good people of Caithness.

Speaking of Georgemas Junction, reminds me of our late stepfather, Lyndesay G. Langwill, who was a railway enthusiast from boyhood. Some years ago my twin brother accompanied Lyndesay on the Georgemas to Thurso line; a brief but memorable experience.

My job was to collect Alan and Lyndesay after their journey. I saw the train on the opposite side of Thurso river: how diminutive it looked against the flat landscape, and the thought struck me, how many on board the train were Caithness exiles, perhaps some of them from the other end of the world?

Maybe some passengers were bound for Orkney, and a sea-crossing was in prospect before they reached kith and kin? One knew not, yet two words might sum it all up: "Quo Vadis"? (Whither goest thou?)

The longest rail journey in Britain used to be that of the "Jellicoe Express" from London to Thurso: it was really for Naval personnel bound for Scapa Flow, but other members of the forces used the train also. Winston Churchill was Prime Minister when he travelled on the "Jellicoe Express".

111

Sir John's Square, Thurso
Photographed by Ronald Thomson.

War Memorial – Thurso.

Thurso Bay.   *Photographed by Dan Mackay.*

THURSO BAY

The sun sets, and a westering breeze
  Blows fresh. I hear a seagull cry
As lonely and with easy grace
  It wings its way. Against the sky
I see the smoke of passing ships
  And cliffs of Orkney glinting red.
Stern Holborn frowns. Long swelling seas
  Roll gently in past Dunnet Head.
And Thurso, silent in the grey
  Of twilight, gazes o'er its bay.

Deep darkness falls. With rising wind
  And lashing rain, once rippling waves
In anger rage. Wide, sweeping rays
  Of light are dimmed, and silent caves
Reverberate. Against the rocks
  The ocean pits its strength. With roar
Like thunder, dashing high it leaps,
  While pebbles chuckle on the shore.
And voices whisper in the light
  Of morn – "A stormy night last night".

And with the sun the waters smile
  Resplendent, foam-tipped, dancing, free.
The sands shine golden. In my heart
  There is a song. Skipping the sea
White winged sea-birds screech in calls
  Of wild defiance. Now I seem
To sink into a reverie of days of
  Yesteryear – and Dream.
And on the wind, faint, full of glee,
  Voices of boyhood welcome me.

Alexander Miller
Caithness Poems.

THURSO AND HOLBORN HEAD
(To David Bruce)

Thurso! Who does not love Thurso? I am a Wicker, of course, and my attachment to the grey old town is abiding; but there are moments when I wish I were a Thursonian. It is impossible to view the superb bay of Thurso, even for the first time, without a sudden sense of admiration, and almost affection. My dear fellow, why should we talk of the Pyramids and the musty Pharaohs when we can come here! I once wrote (and would still write) –

> "Oh thou bonnie Thurso Bay,
>   In my sleep I hear the play
> Of thy chaffing, bluffing surges,
>   Tilting round thy rocks of grey;
> Up the cliffs of dreamland thronging
>   They come answering my longing,
> And their calling woos me back to thee,
>   Thou bonnie Thurso Bay!"

Rather generous from a Wicker – eh! And not a solitary native of Thurso thanked me! It's a tough world for poets, David! They must, like the lairags, sing without sending round the hat!

What wistful, haunting perspectives! How soft and yet reliant are the far-reaching Orkneys! In the evening (for I have been here often), the rarest of all sights are the atmospheric hues which seem to ooze from

Pennyland, Thurso (birthplace of Sir Wm. Smith – Boys' Brigade Founder).
Photographed by Ronald Thomson.

116

headlands and drift over the entire scene, and the dreamy islands appearing to float on an enchanted sea. So have I frequently seen it in early autumn, during some lovely, silent nights.

But it was broad forenoon when Janey and I were there on Tuesday last. We were bound for Holborn Head. Dropping down to the sands we tossed off our boots and paddled, ran, waded, skelped and danced to Scrabster. It was as in the days of the Picts! I hope none of our dandy acquaintants saw us – if we have any! Then (boots on, ye lovers of the Proper!) we rose to the lighthouse – clean, trig and self-sufficient on its rocky pedestal. It is the eye to Holborn's brow. Up – up – to the grassy swell behind, every step a stride into the Pacific Ocean of rarefied air. Blow, blow, ye fresh Pentland winds; blow into our blood the tang of the northern tides and the romance of fair-haired Vikings, and the snore of the gale, and the pelt of the waves in their glee! These, my dear boy, are the influences that endure.

Then on to The Clett – "our great lion", as my loved Robert Dick neatly described it to Hugh Miller. Dick wrote eloquently and affectionately about it, and its impressive grandeur, in his own facile way. He is the Spirit of Holborn Head. All the time we were on it, we talked of him, for Janey is as devoted to his memory as the most loyal

Scrabster – Fishing Port and Gateway to Orkney.
Photographed by Ronald Thomson.

native. It was here that he found some of his favourite flowers; and we had no difficulty in noticing several specimens of the modest little Primula Scotica. Looking at them I recalled the fact that Homer called plants Cheires Theom – "God's hands" – a pretty fancy truly, which you will sanction, I am sure.

Of course, we clambered in to the Deil's Brig and stood facing one of the characteristic views of our Motherland. It is really thrilling to fell yourself in the heart of the rocks, looking through the rude gateway at the big, crunching waves filing the ribs of the coast. Indeed, it makes one shivery with a strange satisfaction.

I think that all Holborn Head may be written of in superlatives. The Brig, the Clett, Slater's Loup, etc. combined make what I should imagine is the most inspiring section of rock-splendour north of the Ord. Do you agree? Anyhow, I feel that just now, with the glories of our ramble strong on my imagination.

We sat down beside the monument at Slater's Loup and turned our telescope on Dunnet Head, with its jagged crevices – studios where wind and weather carve their fantastic subjects. And Dwarwick Head, too, was quite vivid. I think of Calder as the Soul of Dwarwick. His poem on this headland contains two verses which I have always liked, and memorised years ago. Here they are: see what you think of them.

> "Haunt of my boyhood, romantic Dwarwick Head;
>   As on thy bold stupendous form I gaze,
> How vividly, though chequer'd years have fled,
>   Thou wak'st the memory of my school-boy days!
>
> My heart leaps up – I seem once more a boy,
>   And lightly tread thy well-known rugged strand,
> Or climb thy steep and heathy side in joy,
>   With friends long passed into the silent land."

Simple language, and every-day words – and lines that need careful scanning – yet effective, as I think. The present day is not the most liable to remember past work or workers, but I would not like to think of a time when Caithnessians should be indifferent to the talents of Calder.

As we sat resting thus, a tumultuous bumble bee fell with a bang in the grass at our feet – honey-drunk maybe! He was in a great swither and capsized with his momentum. But he seemed to have business on hand. He cooled down in a second or two and took his bearings. Trimming his wings, and looking out steadily as if measuring the distance, he set off across the bay! That's game for you! We followed with our glass the hairy voyager till his sails and hull disappeared. I shall see that bee for many a day yet, and gather courage from him. Rare adventurer!

A saunter across the sands again brought us back to the braehead. We sat long watching the bairns chasing each other in the surf. Rare circus for a tired brain! I think I will conclude my report of our day's outing, at this point – for I would like to sit there for a very long time!

John Horne – Round the Old Home.

A focal point of Thurso is Sir John's Square which prefaces St. Peter's Church. Once known as Macdonald Square, it was renamed in 1893, in honour of Sir John Sinclair of Ulbster (1754-1835). His name will always be linked with the first Statistical Account of Scotland (1792-98) which was his brainchild and which he edited. It was a corporate effort which required data on every parish in Scotland, via the Kirk Minister; this involved 160 queries from nearly 1,000 Ministers and the end result was seven years work and 21 volumes.

Sir John was an MP, a landowner, an economist and a prolific writer. Born at Thurso Castle, he took a strong interest in the "improvement" of Caithness, which was a very backward county. It was Sir John who pioneered the Board of Agriculture, and became its first president. The same who introduced Border sheep to Caithness and called them "Cheviots"; and who laid the blue print for the "New Town" of Thurso, not forgetting the village of Halkirk.

He also took an interest in the fishing industry, via the British Fisheries Board, and championed Wick as a focal point for development. The end result was the new settlement of Pulteneytown, which began the "boom century" in Caithness.

The energy and zeal of Sir John Sinclair caused the Abbe' Gregoire to dub him: "the most indefatigable man in Europe". The portrait of Sir John Sinclair, by Raeburn, reveals the face of a man with a determined look, one who would not be swayed easily from his purpose. In his hand there is a pamphlet, which seems fitting for one who wrote 367 pamphlets on various subjects.

Thurso is journey's end on the British mainland, only the islands beckon further north. Thurso, 21 miles north west of Wick is a pleasant town which had its boom era in the 1950's with the advent of Dounreay, the nuclear energy establishment.

Thurso does not capitalise on its northern aspect, which is surprising in a way, since tourism is important to Caithness. Thurso has the attraction of a fine beach for the holiday-maker, with quick access to Scrabster – the main sea-route to Orkney.

Thurso and Wick are situated at the mouth of a river – Thurso like Wick is an old town: by Royal Charter of Charles I (1633) designated a free burgh of barony, in favour of John, Master of Berriedale. Thurso was a place of some note in ancient times: Historian Torfaeus referred to it as "oppidum Cathnesiae" – the town of Caithness.

Calder's History says that in 1726, Thurso's population was four times that of Wick. Also, that for nearly two centuries, Thurso was the chief seat of the Sheriff Court of Caithness.

In Norse times there was at Ormlie, the Castle of Thurso, a stronghold which the Scandinavian Earls used frequently to reside. As Calder records, not a vestige of the castle remains. The town's name, Thurso, has its origins in the Norse era – "Thor's River" – Thorsa.

It is high summer and I am standing on a narrow country road, a footpath almost, that runs from the Scrabster coastguard hut eventually to join back onto the main Thurso/Scrabster road. I am well above sea level and from about half-way along this road is a spot from which there is so much of beauty for the viewing that the scene is almost breathtaking. The summer sea takes on a gentle aspect with waves rolling calmly on to the shore, seagulls are wheeling along almost at head height, and below on a sandy beach, oystercatchers complete the picture.

From where I am standing I can look directly ahead and see the imposing figure of the "Old Man of Hoy", the famous sea stack, and beyond that the greater part of the Orkneys, visible and mysterious through a slight sea mist, across the Pentland Firth. Looking to the left is Scrabster harbour, full of busy fishing boats, with not a few yards from them, the lifeboat bobbing about reassuringly in the water. The lighthouses at Holborn and Dunnet Heads give immense charm and character to the scene as only lighthouses can, while hiding their real purpose just as the sea hides the ferocious rocks of the coastline, a perpetual unseen danger to shipping.

Just a few months ago, spring was bringing its own unique visual rewards, for with its showers and sunshine it can produce rainbows which span the whole bay, showing colours of almost blinding intensity. At this time, the hills above the lighthouse are rich with the sights and sounds of spring. Covered in daffodils, primroses and celandines, yellow predominates and when the fields of the farms on the hill beyond Scrabster are full of lambs, the picture of spring is complete.

It is autumn now, with the darker evenings, so that the whole scene changes. In the harbour the fishing boats are ablaze with lights looking like numerous Christmas trees. As the lights of Scrabster diffuse into the sea, it almost seems to be on fire, alight with an orange glow. A rare jewel on a cold clear autumn night is a sight of the Merry Dancers (the Aurora Borealis, or Northern Lights). The heavens are illuminated with a range of pastel hues in a continually changing picture, quite unlike anything else nature can offer.

A few months later and it is winter, and even this inhospitable season can be beautiful with the distant Orkneys showing snow covered hills. The gentle waves of summer have changed to menacing rollers demonstrating all their might and majesty. In spite of the weather, the fishing boats still put to sea, often flooding like small corks, dwarfed by massive waves. As I look again at the lifeboat, I know just what may be expected of her gallant crew in these conditions.

This is indeed my favourite Caithness view, and having spent most of my life in crowded, noisy, dusty London, this is something to be treasured. No wonder this spot has become almost hallowed to me. How come you may ask, can I be around at so many times and seasons?

My secret is a simple one. I am lucky enough to see all that I have described from my front garden. It is often quoted that "home is where the heart is" and truly, mine is firmly planted in Caithness.

Mrs Florence E. Wymans
East Gill, Scrabster.
This essay won first prize in the Alan Thomson Memorial Competition:
My favourite Caithness view.

SCRABSTER

R. L. Stevenson's timeless quote about "hanging round harbour sides is the richest form of idling" strikes a chord about Scrabster: it has an attractive character which draws the visitor back, situated as it is on the west side of Thurso Bay.

Scrabster is not only the home port for Thurso, but also the principal gateway to Orkney, and the "St. Ola" makes daily crossings from Scrabster to Stromness. For many, the crossing is an experience, given the Pentland Firth's reputation.

Scrabster is well worth a visit, not only to soak up local colour, but to admire the splendour of Thurso Bay. Hugh Miller of Cromarty fame, considered Thurso Bay the finest in Britain, and John Horne reckoned it was best seen at sundown:

"When the waves slip and shimmer over the rocky ledges and waltz to their haunts again, and the Head of Holborn is laced in shadow, and Dunnet Head is sculptured by the setting sun, and the Orkney Islands seem to float, and all the sea and sky are mystic shadowland."

Try the view above Holborn Head Lighthouse, on a fine summer day, and you will experience the magic of Caithness: the full sweep of Thurso

Bay lies calm and benevolent as a sabbath morn, while Orkney beckons northward, casting its own spell.

Holborn Head has some of the finest cliff-scenery you could wish for – at first sight breath-taking – in its rugged grandeur. But have a care if you seek out this haunt of seabirds, this primeval piece of Caithness, for those are steep towering cliffs which rise from the deep blue-green sea at Holborn. Caution then must be the keynote.

An evening cruise from Scrabster on the St. Ola! How inviting the prospect on a night of brilliant sunshine, when Orkney's sandstone cliffs beckoned with a colourful, mystic presence – the lure was undeniably northward with a calm sea as bonus.

Strange to witness Dunnet Head from the St. Ola, and see it loom above us, a fitting end to mainland Scotland. There it stood like a natural fortress with its lighthouse atop, a guardian of old under the August sun.

The sway and pitch of the St. Ola made one aware of the living sea below us, that very sea which holds so many secrets in its bosom. Hardy are those who sail to Orkney in defiance of weather, sometimes of course, the elements defy the best of ships and mariners, and the St. Ola is storm bound at Stromness her home port.

The Norsemen knew the Pentland Firth as the "Pentland Fiord" – the very name may be Pictish in origin: Pictland or Pentland Firth. Thus a cruise on this famous sea lane is something of a history lesson in itself and a reminder of Viking days.

In August 1263, Haco, King of Norway, set sail from St Margaret's Hope, Orkney to fight the Scottish King, Alexander III. Imagine the scene as Haco's fleet entered the Pentland Firth with more than 100 ships: the King's own ship, the Royal Galley, was large and fashioned entirely from oak.

"Its dragon head glowed with burnished gold: the banner of Norway was displayed at the stern, and the warrior champions were ranged along the deck in proud array." [1]

The Battle of Largs, on the west coat of Scotland, was a disaster for the Norse King. He lost 160 of his men and the greater part of his fleet was destroyed by a tempest. Historian Calder says that King Haco died of a broken heart in the bishop's palace at Kirkwall, and his remains were taken to Bergen, Norway for a royal funeral.

Back to our cruise again: a close-up view of the "Old Man of Hoy" was impressive, if somewhat daunting in the retreating light. This pinnacle rises from the sea to a height of 450 feet. Many a day we saw it from our

---

[1] *Calder's History of Caithness.*

Holborn Head Lighthouse, Thurso Bay.

Photographed by Dan Mackay.

Caithness home when it appeared like a raised finger on the distant horizon.

The present St. Ola is the third of that title on the Scrabster – Stromness route (28 nautical miles) and the ship's name derives from the patron saint of Norway, St. Olaf, who died in 1030, when Orkney was a Norse province.

Those unfamiliar with the Pentland Firth might like to know it is from six to eight miles broad and some 16 miles in length, notable for its rapid tidal currents plus dangerous reefs and eddies.

It is said that on a clear night, nine lighthouses plus two beacons can be seen from Duncansby Head.

The Pentland Firth has enough legends to match its moods and is as potent a symbol of the Far North as the rugged winds which sear across its face and dash its spray above the rocks.

Halkirk and Watten are the only inland villages in Caithness. The blueprint for Halkirk belongs to Sir John Sinclair of Ulbster, who designed the village on generous lines, and even today Halkirk has a spacious look, with neatly laid streets.

Halkirk is very much a venue for the fisherman, for as well as Thurso river, the parish is notable for some 24 lochs, enough to keep the most ardent angler busy!

Halkirk was a place of note in ancient times, being the seat of the Bishopric of Caithness until 1222 – the very name of Halkirk (Norse: Ha Kirkja) denotes "High Church". The Castle of Brawl, once known as "Brathwell" had been dated to 1375 – this tower or keep – now in ruins – was, according to Calder, the occasional residence of the Scandinavian Earls of Orkney and Caithness, and was probably erected by one of them.

The ancient name of the Parish was St. Fergus and St. Thomas and there were chapels at Skinnet, Banniskirk and Spittal. At Spittal was the Gunn cemetery, last resting place of their chiefs and principal men.

A focal point of Halkirk today is the north end of the village with its fine War Memorial: that of a widow looking down on her boy, her hand on his head, and the figures sculptured in white marble bear testimony to the sorrow of war. The Memorial stands by the Thurso river which happily knows nothing of wars and bloodshed, and man's inhumanity to man, but continues on its peaceful way.

Those who seek a contrast to the coastal villages of Caithness, might care to visit Halkirk, and then perhaps discover some of the hinterland which lies beyond.

No signpost marks the way to Dirlot where the Thurso river flows through picturesque scenery near Westerdale. This beauty spot is well

off the beaten track and may be regarded a gem of Caithness.
You drive through a quarry, stop by the first house, then cross a field where the landmark is a small isolated cemetery. Alas, it is a run-down neglected place, notable for memorials with the surname Gunn.
But the attraction here is the river below: living, vibrant, alive! The dark river flows with a will, tumbling over rocks, drawing the eye downstream. Sheep graze in this precinct where only man seems like an intruder, and primroses star the banks of the river, lovely in their solitude.
Dirlot may be likened to a miniature gorge, and therein lies much of its appeal; certainly it presents an ideal composition for the artist or photographer. Dirlot Castle has long disappeared in the mists of antiquity, but its location on a steep crag must have been impressive. The Keep was small, but the site notable, and it was inland – something unusual in Caithness.
The original owner is believed to have been Reginald or Ronald Cheyne, a Caithness chieftain, whose lands included nearly a third of the county. Calder noted in his history that "the lands in Caithness seem to have been conferred on the Cheynes by charter from David II. The name as originally spelt in Norman French, was Du Cheyne."
In days bygone, there was bloodshed at Dirlot Castle (the result of clan feuds) but all that belongs to the dim and distant past, what remains is a peaceful scene: an intriguing picture, Highland in character, where the river is always supreme.

R.T.

Westerdale – Thurso River.   *Photographed by Ronald Thomson.*

MOORLAND MAGIC

The vacant moor stretches out
  Robed in purple hue;
A warm breeze stirs
  The nearby silver loch,
A peace beyond time
  Touches the soul anew.

In this primeval land
  Of russett sandstone cliffs,
That border the Pentland sea,
  The sun kissed lochans
Mirror floating clouds
  That belong to no one.

Grand those placid images
  Bathed in morning light,
And the sweet incense
  Of heather, a rich nectar;
In this superb scene
  The peace of God is nigh.

Ronald Thomson.

DISTANCES

I would rave about Cattiland were it only for its moorlands. How remoteness, in his subjects. He opened the gateways of infinity by introducing gradations of distance and aerial perspective. He made canvas talk to the imagination as well as to the eye. (Keats wrote a poem on his "Enchanted Castle".) What unlimited inducements he would have found in Cattiland! Had he painted the Lochmore heatherland, with the sierras of Scaraben and its attendants searching the sky at the far line of vision, Keats would have lost his wits in trying to interpret it! Yet, here is the scene itself, laid out with more realism than Claude or any other human genius could have presented; and with ever-varying conditions, too. And it waits in all its swart magnaninity for our wonder and pleasure!

This is ancientry, if you will! It is the burial-place of centuries. And it unfolds itself in lavish rusticity. "Immensity" is not the word for it, and "range" is lacking in verisimilitude. No word quite hits it for me: the high-sounding ones exaggerate and the common ones belittle.

The last time I was there I grew from an admirer to a devotee. There was a chancy wind snuffling among the heather, and scutching the riverface as if in frolic. It was a warm wind, for the sun was hot and the moor seemed to perspire. A tenuous, misty heat vibrated the atmosphere and gave that effect of softness to the scene that artists get by half-closing the eyes and looking at their work through the mesh of their eyelashes. I could feel all this, and riot in it; but I need not try to transfer the sensations by the medium of words. Fortunately, the experience is not uncommon. When I came away, it was with unwilling steps. I gazed again and again across the wide vastitude at venerable Morven, while the clouds wove scarves like Shetland lace around its shoulders; and I thought not even Claude, nor our own Constable, had succeeded in suggesting a finer sense of distance.

The same moor looks neglected enough sometimes. I have seen it on dour, frosty days when it seemed to be suffering from illness; and on days of drench, when everything looked weary and pathetic, and I have noticed the winter scowl on Morven as ugsome as any untamed fancy might desire. Even then, realism had its grim opportunity; and the moorland grandeur was only changed from the sombre to the austere. The purple of the heather was bleached (rusty, sienna-like), and weather gave another complexion to the plain; but it had still its own shaggy, unequivocal appeal. (I am not sure but Rob Roy was a fitter subject for the brush after a fight than after a wash!) Anyhow, in all seasons it preserves its own proud and careless supremacy and is never at any time lacking in the great quality of impressiveness.

Any representative scene of Cattiland must include it. And were I asked where such view might be obtained, I would say, "From Hoy Station". The village of Halkirk lies in front, and its old and new castles

Old Mill at Forss. *Photographed by Dan Mackay.*

succeeded in suggesting a finer sense of distance.

The same moor looks neglected enough sometimes. I have seen it on dour, frosty days when it seemed to be suffering from illness; and on days of drench, when everything looked weary and pathetic, and I have noticed the winter scowl on Morven as ugsome as any untamed fancy might desire. Even then, realism had its grim opportunity; and the moorland grandeur was only changed from the sombre to the austere. The purple of the heather was bleached (rusty, sienna-like), and weather gave another complexion to the plain; but it had still its own shaggy, unequivocal appeal. (I am not sure but Rob Roy was a fitter subject for the brush after a fight than after a wash!) Anyhow, in all seasons it preserves its own proud and careless supremacy and is never at any time lacking in the great quality of impressiveness.

Any representative scene of Cattiland must include it. And were I asked where such view might be obtained, I would say, "From Hoy Station". The village of Halkirk lies in front, and its old and new castles – characteristic and typical of the county; to the east, this big breast of Cattiland, flecked with cultivated fields and houses of varying importance, spreads out for many miles: and beyond all, far at the back of everything, the profiles of Morven and Scaraben rise into the sky, solemn and imposing. This, I think, is our most inclusive view.

John Horne.
"Summer Days in Cattiland."

There are paintings which reflect Caithness in a special way; sometimes it may be a landscape scene which conveys the spacious element, pleasing the eye, and stirring memory toward the individual beauty of the northland.

On the other hand, it may be an intimate view which invites admiration. A notable example is Samuel Birch's evocative picture of the Forss River: "A Haunt of Ancient Peace, the Forss River, Thurso". How well the artist depicted this beauty spot, some five and a half miles on the A836 Thurso to Dounreay road.

A painting may give pleasure as a work of art, yet surely the imprint is deeper and more notable when the locale is known and appreciated. Thus the Forss picture appealed to me, reviving memories of summer visits to this place of river and trees and disused mill where the vibrant water cascades down its miniature staircase, in timeless fashion.

An Edinburgh Caithness friend, the late George McLeod's yardstick of a good painting was whether he could live with a picture or not; well, there's no doubt he would have cherished the Forss picture!

The viewpoint looking downstream on a summer day certainly made an ideal composition for Samuel Birch RA (1869-1955) and the end result is impressive indeed.

The flat, bare, landscape of Caithness has an individual beauty, again one coins the word – spacious – there is something epic in its appeal; conversely, the attraction of the Forss scene is in its character and compactness – a Caithness gem.

Unforgettable too, must be the sight of a salmon leaping upstream at Forss Falls, that split second of triumph, which has a timeless quality also.

St Mary's Chapel, Crosskirk, is thought to be the oldest church ruin in Caithness, a remnant of the 12th Century. Thus a walk to this outpost via the Forss water is a reminder of bygone days. Sheep graze by the small cemetery which enfolds the ruin, a small stark place whose existence on the Christian map is no doubt what mattered.

The Department of the Environment has decreed it a protected site and informs the visitor that the low doorway in the east and west walls of the Nave are reminders of early Christian and romanesque architecture.

It cannot have been easy for the early Christian missionaries – a number of whom came from Ireland – to begin the work of the Celtic Church – but they scattered spiritual seed which took root in the flat land of Caithness.

John Horne, writing of those Gospel pioneers, has mentioned their "heroic qualities of faith and courage and sacrifice". On the roll call of the dedicated their names are evergreen.

Those who wish to visit Crosskirk should take the A836 Thurso to Dounreay road and turn right at Forss crossroads till they reach the end of a minor road. Thereafter the journey continues on foot – it is a pleasant walk enhanced by the river which has almost reached the sea.

Below Crosskirk is great slanting rock scenery which preface the restless sea, and cliffs of Orkney loom on the horizon with exotic colours to inspire the best of artists. That alone makes a journey to Crosskirk worthwhile on a summer day.

THE BARD OF REAY

Whenever I think of that brooding area between Loch Inchard and Cape Wrath, the face of a dead and forgotten poet comes into my mind's eye. They called him The Bard of Reay. He was Henry Henderson, sub-postmaster at Dounreay long before the dome of an atomic reactor dominated the landscape – and what he would have said about that gleaming symbol of man's progress, God only knows. He was 81 years old when I first met him in his house, but he had the strength of two there isn't a grey hair on my head. Look at it!" he grabbed a handful of his thick, unkempt hair and yanked it roughly.

All his life, the Bard of Reay had been writing poetry. A lot of it had been scribbled on bits of wrapping paper. Some of it had been printed in the "Caithness Courier", none at all outside the county. He was the most cheerful and unrewarded rhymer who ever lived in Scotland. He made no complaints and spoke well of everybody.

People told me that the Bard never went to school, but they were wrong. He attended a school in Dounreay until he was 20 – because he had to start late – and was taken pretty deeply into Latin, algebra and astronomy by Thomas Bryers, an ill-paid dominie who had come up from Dumfriesshire. He studied so hard in fact, that he had a breakdown and for his health's

The Bard o' Reay.

131

sake he quit books and laboured on the land.

His mother was a Morrison from the country around Loch Inchard, and one of his poems which took my fancy was a nostalgic tribute to that corner of Scotland, it concluded:

"An' if I e'er should pass that way,
    I would be fain to tarry;
And spend a long midsummer's day,
    In bonnie Strath Sinairidh;
And watch the mist of eventide,
    With bridal veilings drape;
The hills and mountains in their pride,
    'Twixt Inchard and The Cape."

I am not a poet, and the poetic pundits of modern Scotland would scarcely consider me qualified to sharpen their precious pencils, but I got something out of that artless rhyme which may, perhaps, have been put into it by the mysterious ingredient of language which clothes commonplace words with feeling and beauty. So ends my tribute to my friend, the Bard of Reay.

John Herries McCulloch,
The Charm of Scotland.

Seeking out people at grass roots, and casting a fresh slant on the byways of Scotland, was very much the essence of J.H. McCulloch's writing – for 25 years he was a footloose staff writer of the Scottish Daily Express.

A WALK IN CAITHNESS

Once over the brow of Brabsterdorran
There is a straight mile down the ribboned road
Pink and lilac-hued under this cool September sun.
Morning rain refreshed the rolling fields,
Swimming in limelights and sunspots, treeless,
Rolling from us, the child and me.
Dark gauzes shuffle and lift on the mountains beyond.
Blue the pyramid tombs of ancient Celtic kings.
All lost and dead in Sutherland, lost and passed
Feather hedged diamonds slide into Stemster,
The sleeping form of a green harlequin,
And the shadow of light slipping up the road
Towards us as we go down. This remains.
The light, the space, the road
And a child sliding in and out of dreams.

Elizabeth McArdle.

MAGIC OF CAITHNESS

ALEXANDER MILLER

The rich Caithness tongue – so familiar to one's forebears – still lives in the poetry of Alexander Miller (1900-45). Take for example the first verse of his poem "IF":

> "If blackchock fustles on a tree
> If sprowgie cheeps lek fit till dee
> If gullag skirls ower angry sea
> Till me they're Kaitness."

Here it seems is the heartbeat, the rhythm of the old dialect, indeed the couthy, homespun words are unmistakably "Kaitness". Think again of that verse: this time substitute blackbird for blackchock, whistles for fustles, sparrow for sprowgie, gull for gullag and Caithness for Kaitness. Now compare the two. Which do you prefer?

Certainly the old words reflect the Caithness heritage in vivid form. Anglicise those words and the essential character is lost. Dialect poetry – such as Alex Miller wrote – should for best effect be recited. A classic example of dialect verse is Burns' "Tam O' Shanter", which is a great poem read, but an experience heard.

Words familiar and unfamiliar crop up in Alex Miller's poetry: "peedie" (small), "hammal" (homely), "chiel" (person) on one side, and "scuttered" (did something awkwardly), "scrammelt" (scrambled) and "smyaggert" (soiled) on the other – the latter almost qualify as tongue twisters!

Writing in his mother's tongue, he caught the Caithness character with shrewd, sometimes humorous insight, and the memorial booklet: "Caithness Poems of Alexander Miller" (Caithness Books) reflects his pithy style.

Trained as a reporter, Alex Miller became northern representative of the "People's Journal", at Inverness. He was born in Glasgow to Caithness parents – yet it was Thurso he regarded as home – the Miller family returned north when Alex was eight. The questing days of boyhood were never forgotten – especially the summer days.

> "Fan bit a peedie loon
> Wi' a' 'e ither boyagies
> A scuttered roon 'e toon
> A gang o' ringan deevils."

Thus his nostalgic poem: "Fan We Were Young" has an authentic ring, a flavour of boyhood in its prime. His ability to convey mood comes over strongly in the aptly titled: "Thirsa".

THURSO AND BEYOND

"Near a peedie house a rowan
  Grows. 'Ere's a boolies at 'e door,
An' a peat fire luntan, lowan,
  Castan shadows 'cross 'e floor,
Wi' a sound 'at's growan, growan
  O' 'e wave-beats on 'e shore.
At Thirsa."

Another example is from his poem "Desires" – the lines are simple yet effective.

"A lek til see 'e burns in speite,
  An' feel 'e kiss o' spring,
Till watch 'e peedie sprowgies meite,
  An' follow 'a on wing.

A lek til dander ower 'e hill,
  An' smell 'e mornin' breeze,
Til hear 'e lairag's risan trill,
  An' softly lappan seas.

A lek til sit on autumn nichts,
  Fan twilicht's creepan doon,
An' see 'e flichtran fairy lichts
  Blink oot a' ower 'e toon."

"Kirk-goan in Winter" is probably Alex Miller's most notable poem in the vernacular. Those familiar with the poem will recall the young man who would rather have lain "snowg in bed" than face the rigour of winter-cold and going to Kirk. However, his mother had other ideas! The writing is crisp, the images life-like, and the poem, surely a comment on human nature!

Incidentally, the man who wrote dialect poetry, also wrote one of his most evocative poems in "English": "Thurso Bay" (see elsewhere in this book).

Perhaps like R. L. Stevenson, Alex Miller wrote his own epitaph when he penned the following lines:

"Brooding and mist-tipped hills are not for me,
  Reverberating glens, nor forests deep.
Give me a virgin heath, a wind swept lea
  Near beetling crags. There let me sleep
With me and mine in Caithness."

Tribute has been paid of the spirit in which he wrote, and above all lived, during those latter years when he was "dogged by chronic ill-health". His untimely death at 40, left a void in Caithness writing. Much water has flown down Thurso River since the "hammal" words held sway in Caithness, yet the homespun lines of Alexander Miller, may serve as a memory of the "Kaitness" he knew and loved.

R.T. John O'Groat Journal

He was a much-travelled man, and before I left Thurso he told me that The Causeymire (short for Causeway Mire), which runs through the great bog of that name in Caithness, was the most desolate road on the face of the earth.

"It's terrible", he said. "You'll see."

Well, I didn't tell him that I had already driven over the road more than once, but he was right up to a point. The Causeymire on a wintry day, with snow in the air and no traffic moving, can be very desolate and even frightening.

And that day, in less than 15 minutes after leaving Thurso, I was a lone figure in a lifeless landscape dotted with the crumbling ruins of forgotten crofts and the mysterious brochs, hut circles and tumuli which tell us that a primitive race once lived on that prairie of peat.

There is no other area of comparable size in this country which is so desolate, for by my reckoning it must have an area of at least 50 square miles. Even the mountains of Sutherland seem scared of it, for the peaks of Morven, Maiden Pap and Scaraben just peep over its distant rim.

The Causeymire was built in 1772 by Sir John Sinclair of Statistical Account fame, when he was only 18 years old. He must have been a persuasive young wizard, for he got 1,260 suspicious crofters, farmers and landlords together, convinced them that the road through the great bog was necessary, and got them to build it. It is difficult to imagine a youth of 18 organising and carrying through such a project of self-help in modern Scotland.

It would be impossible to get 1,260 men together in the Causeymire region today for any purpose whatsoever. In fact, you would have to walk a long way to find a dozen, and you might be talking to yourself before you got around to them all.

There were evictions from that area too in the old days, and they were carried out with more than the usual display of arrogance and stupidity. It was the old Scottish story all over again – the emigration of the sturdy native stock, empty crofts, and desolation spreading in a big way. When one gets right into the Causeymire, away from the road, there are more brochs than houses; just an awful lot of nothing as the old man at Latheron put it.

John Herries McCulloch
The Charm of Scotland.

Old Keiss Castle, Caithness – Site of 1st Baptist Church in Scotland, 1750.
Photographed by Ronald Thomson.

SAUCER OVER STRUPSTER

She was mad, she told herself, stark, staring, raving mad, – well not raving perhaps, but certainly crazy to be out walking across the heather in the middle of a chill October night. She knew exactly where she was going, but not why. She was heading for Strupster, to a farmhouse standing exactly three miles from anywhere – right in the middle of the heather. She knew perfectly well that she could have walked along the county road for some distance, and then have turned left up the rough road, and have reached the place in a much easier manner, but instinctively she knew that her mission, whatever it was, must be kept secret.

She was thankful for the intermittent gleams of moonlight which helped to light her way, and also for the scudding clouds which darkened the moon and hid her from view. It was not an unknown short cut. She had taken it many times in daylight when she went to help with the animals which the owner of the farm kept around the place. No one lived in the farmhouse, but she knew where the key was kept, and often she had gone inside to make a meal or a cup of tea.

It was strange that she did not feel cold, and then she realised that she was wearing warm tweeds, her wellington boots, and a thick quilted blue anorak, with the hood covering her head and fastened at the neck. She had not worn it since that day when Peter had gone away – never to return. The car taking him to the airport had broken down, and there had been no time for any fond farewell by the time they got a lift and reached Wick. One telephone message when he had reached his destination in England, and then nothing more. A test pilot, his plane had disintegrated somewhere over the sea, and nothing had ever been found. That was five years ago. It had seemed like an eternity of heartbreak and anguish – years when it had seemed that she had walked in a Sahara of loneliness. If only they had been able to say "Good-bye!"

Margaret, for that was her name, crossed several fences, jumped several ditches, and skirted the old peat banks, till she came in sight of a small cottage. Here old Kirsty dwelt, and dwelt is the word, for the old thatched cottage was just as it had been in Kirsty's grandmother's day. No "mod-cons" for her, but she was perfectly content, growing her own vegetables in a little patch at the back of the house, baking her own bannocks over a peat fire, and if she did not have a cow nowadays, well there was always condensed milk to be had. Even the tin-opener she possessed was a very ancient one with a lion's head on it. Her sole companion was her collie dog, now getting old, like Kirsty herself.

Margaret fervently hoped that the dog was safely in the house and not out of doors, where he would soon find her and start barking. She had no wish to frighten Kirsty, nor to reveal her presence.

She had just managed to tiptoe past the cottage when she heard a sound that made her feel as if her hair stood on end. Kirsty's dog was howling! Long, low, blood-curdling howls. Margaret stood rooted to the spot. After what seemed an incredibly long time, silence descended once more. She hurried on, and now she felt more than a little afraid. She tried to calm her nerves by picturing her surroundings as she knew them in daylight – the gold of the cornfields for the harvest was late that year, the blue of the sea and sky, the purple of the heather, the steely glitter of the little lochans, the comforting sight of sheep, cows, horses, hens and ducks, and the voices of well kent loved ones. But that seemed another world and another life.

At last the steading at Strupster came into view, and as she reached the door and took the key from its hiding place, she felt the old familiar feeling of belonging, a feeling that this was home. For many times she had found that three miles from anywhere can be a haven of peace.

Margaret opened the door, went inside, and sat down. Everything was deadly silent. She was waiting. But for whom or what? She sat, neither afraid nor unafraid – just waiting. No clock ticked. There was no fire in the grate to make a cheerful sound. There was no lamplight, although all she had to do was to stretch out her hand and reach for the lamp and matches which always sat on the table. But she did not move.

The clouds had cleared away for the time being and the moonlight shone right through the window. It touched her hair with a halo of silvery light.The door still stood open. It seemed to her that she was alone on the earth and waiting.

Suddenly the air became electric, and she felt shivers of excitement running down her back. There was a low humming, vibrating sound in the air. Slowly and surely the sound became louder in her ears and then became so high pitched that she could not hear it any more. Then again there was a faint low humming vibrating sound – and a luminosity filling the window and the door-way.

It seemed to Margaret that she held her breath for a long time, and then let it out with a low gasp. For, filling the doorway and coming into the room, was a figure dressed in some sort of uniform which was close fitting and covered him completely. He seemed to float towards her slowly, for it did not seem as if his feet touched the ground. Only his face was visible.

"Peter! Peter!" she cried as she walked towards him and flung herself into his arms. He kissed her eyes, her mouth, her hair and then, as Peter had always done, he kissed the tip of her nose. They gazed deeply into each other's eyes, and then, just as mysteriously as he had come into the room, just as mysteriously he vanished. For the life of her she could not move. She knew that whatever agency, human or otherwise, had brought him to Strupster, it was already taking him away, to the accompaniment of the strange supersonic sounds she had heard before. The luminous quality of the atmosphere faded away, and it seemed to her that now in its place there was the first faint hint of dawn.

Margaret walked from the room, locked the door and replaced the key in its secret niche. She knew she would have to return the way she had come and she only hoped that she would get home and back into bed without anyone being the wiser. She felt happier than she had felt for a long long time.

When she passed Kirsty's cottage the dog was whining. Had the Angel of Death crossed the threshold and left him alone? Margaret went across to the door and whispered "It's all right, Carlo! Everything is all right." The whining ceased. She hurried on as best as she could, sometimes stumbling over the tussocks of heather, for now she was beginning to feel tired and sleepy. Also she could feel one or two spots of rain on her face. She decided to go into the house through the front door and reach her bedroom by way of the parlour, thankful for once that two separate doors led into her room. Luck was with her as no one wakened up to hear of her nocturnal rambles, and just to make sure that no one found out, she hid her anorak, her tweed skirt, and her wellington boots in the little cupboard below her window. Soon she was sound asleep.

Back up in Kirsty's cottage Carlo too was asleep, comforted by a known voice and the knowledge that he was not wholly bereft.

At Strupster the rain battered down on the ground relentlessly, obliterating all traces of the strange visitant and the still stranger craft which had brought him.

Of course for some considerable time there would be people who would speak of a flying saucer over Strupster, – but then who would believe them?

Jane Thomson Langwill.
Edinburgh Caithness Magazine.

HALKIRK MEMOIR

It had been a fine summer day bearing out John Horne's sentiment that when you get a good day in Caithness it's a pearl.

Our venue for high tea was Halkirk, that quiet village by the Thurso River. While tea was being made, we lingered by the bridge and admired the view downstream. A solitary horse caught our eye as it grazed on the river-bank. The scene was idyllic under a warm sun.

We ate alone in a dining room adorned with some antique portraits –

the pictures were low key with muted colours, perhaps faded by time and sunlight. The 18th century figures, sober looking men, may well have been landowners and likely enough be related.

Outside again, the sun had not lost its strength, and a stroll by the riverside, seemed an attractive idea. Some youngsters were soaking up the sun as we walked upstream. Mid-stream, knots of yellow flowers, created a focal point of their own.

The picturesque river might well have been in a Caithness tourist magazine, or northern calendar. And the beauty of this Halkirk gem, was its ease of access for the visitor.

A little further along the scene opened to the hinterland of Caithness, attractive in the evening sun. Miles away the great inland plateau of the flow country, intriguingly dubbed, "the last great wilderness in Europe" could be found.

Our short stroll by the Thurso River, was truly the magic of Caithness, and another red-letter day among Caithness memories.

R.T.

MORNING OF THY DAY

This is the morning of Thy Day,
  And what a lovely autumn morn!
What peace rests on the Hills of Reay,
  And on the fields of ripening corn.

There was a day of old, in Reay,
  A milestone on the way to heaven;
What loving trysts were kept that day,
  What gratitude for sins forgiven.

And pilgrims came from far away,
  To hold communion with their friends;
Foretasting of the happy day,
  The joyful tryst, that never ends.

With heartfelt rapture did they come,
  Forgetting all their worldly care;
They left their all to follow Him,
  And to His footstool to repair.

From ivory gates, the saintly Cooks,
  Came with the message of His love;
With heavenly fragrance in their looks,
  And sweet communion from above.

141

And many a contrite heart came there,
And found in Gilead a balm;
Yes, found rest in the house of prayer,
And soul refreshment in the Psalm.

What people came to Reay that day!
Some came on horseback, some in carts;
And some came barefoot all the way,
With warm and cheerful hearts.

They found a welcome everywhere,
To every guest they were the same;
A welcome table spread with fare,
And plenty beds for all who came.

Where has that loving kindness gone:
The hearts that welcomed all? I say;
More guests were then in every home
Than are within our kirks today.

They loved, and they were loved again,
They bravely footed Life's rough road;
They had their shares of grief and pain,
All children of one Loving God.

Donald Mackay.

Donald Mackay writes in **This Was My Glen:** *The first week in August was known all over the Northern Counties as the Reay Communion.*

"NAVIGATION. MAGICAL STONES OF THE SUN"
"Reprinted by permission from TIME, The Weekly Newsmagazine; Copyright Time Inc. 1967"

Without benefit of compass, Viking sailors of the 9th century managed to ply their watery routes of conquest and commerce, navigating by stars at night and by sun during the day. No matter what the weather, according to ancient Scandinavian sagas, the sun could always be located with the aid of magical "sun stones". Summarising sunstone lore in a recent article in the archaeology magazine Skalk, Danish Archaeologist, Thorkild Ramskou, lamented that none of the sagas clearly describe the sun stone. "But there seems to be a possibility", he wrote, "that it was an instrument which in clouded weather could show where the sun was." Now, with a clue supplied by a young archaeology enthusiast, Ramskou has discovered the secret of the sun-seeking stones of the ancients.

To the 10-year-old son of Jorgen Jensen, chief navigator of the Scandinavian Airlines System, the instrument described in Skalk sounded much like the twilight compass used by his father on flights at high latitudes, where the magnetic compass is unreliable. The twilight compass is equipped with a Polaroid filter that enables a navigator to locate the position of the sun – even when it is behind clouds or below the horizon – by the sun light polarized by the atmosphere.

Flight Test. Intrigued by his son's observation, Jensen passed it on to Ramskou, who immediately recognised its scientific implication. Enlisting the aid of Denmark's royal-court jeweller, the archaeologist collected minerals found in Scandinavia whose molecules are all aligned parallel to each other, just as the crystals are in a Polaroid filter. Ramskou found that one of these minerals, a transparent crystal called cordierite, turned from yellow to dark blue whenever its natural molecular alignment was held at right angles to the plane of polarized light from the sun. Thus, he reasoned, a Viking could have located the sun by rotating a chunk of cordierite until it turned dark blue.

Putting cordierite to the test, Ramskou accompanied Navigator Jensen on an SAS flight to Greenland, keeping track of the sun with his stone while Jensen used the twilight compass. His observations were accurate to within $2\frac{1}{2}°$ of the sun's true position, and he was able to track the sun until it had dipped $7°$ below the horizon. "I now feel convinced," Ramskou concludes, "that the old Viking sailors with the aid of their sun stones could navigate with enormous accuracy."

"Caithness continued subject to Norwegian rule for nearly 400 years" – Calder's History of Caithness.

CHAPTER 7
THE MAGIC OF CAITHNESS

It was one of those bright windy days when the sea is restless, only the gulls seemed indifferent to the wind, as they patrolled the shore with a beady eye. It was late September in Caithness, and autumn graced the land. Despite the wind, the pulse of nature was slowing up, rest was at hand.

The last visitors made occasional forays here and there; in a Thurso bookshop, a Dutchman asked for literature on Thurso, a guidebook; he called the burgh "a pretty town". No, he had not heard of his countryman, Jan de Groot, but agreed he must return and investigate.

The Dutch visitor would have enjoyed the view of Sinclair's Bay, on the braehead above Keiss harbour, for the composition is ideal. The full sweep of the Bay lies before you, enhanced by the sunlit sea; while below the braehead is the little harbour, a refuge from those stormy seas.

All this is Caithness to the core, a timeless, resplendent scene, which has mood, vitality, and the expressive power of nature. Keiss village is well worth a visit for this view alone.

Given a windy day, there is the compensation of great cloud pictures, majestic and transient. And Caithness, so flat and bare, is the ideal county to watch them. The waning year has its own appeal, for the fields have yielded their harvest and stand mellow under the autumn sun. Rich indeed the divine promise which says: "While the earth remaineth, seed time and harvest will not fail."

Even the moorland, though its glory is shed, presents an attractive picture under the retreating sun.

That doyen of Caithness writers, John Horne (1861-1934) left some superb pen pictures of his native county. Take for example "Round the Old Home" (1935) which may be regarded as a collector's piece for Caithness exiles.

The book, edited by his daughter, Janey Horne Robertson, contains letters and speeches of the popular author and Baptist Minister who became a leading light with the Glasgow Caithness Association.

Those holiday letters to family and friends offer fascinating glimpses of the Caithness John Horne knew and loved.

A favourite haunt was Reay parish, not least for its hills: "There are baby hills you can saunter over to get an appetite for your dinner; and there are hills in full manhood that require a day to interview satisfactorily."

With two companions he climbed Ben Ratha, on a day when the "sea was motionless with the weight of sunshine" and found it a memorable experience.

His recall of a place, a scene, a moment, reveals the keen eye of a literary craftsman. Yet there was nothing pretentious about his writing, only the desire to share something which inspired him about Caithness.

In another letter to his wife, John Horne writes in praise of Robert Dick, the notable Thurso baker and geologist, whose botanical knowledge of Caithness was second to none.

Robert Dick's discovery of the "Holy Grass" by the Thurso River was a unique find in its day, but what attracted John Horne was Robert Dick's secret fernery.

The secluded location appealed to John Horne and prompted him to write: "The spot is simply idyllic. You must come to see it next time you visit Reay."

John Horne records that a walk from Wick to Sibster was never absent from his holiday programme. The return walk, via the riverside, revealed a profusion of wild flowers "flashing to senses many impressive hints of nature's unsophisticated beauty and universal variety."

Louisburgh Street, Wick was the birthplace of John Horne. In his day, the town was the great herring centre of Scotland. The epic novel of those herring fishers came from another Caithness writer, Neil Gunn in the "Silver Darlings" published in 1941.

A favourite haunt of John Horne was the North Head at Wick. He reckoned Thurso Bay was noble indeed, but "if you want a horizon come to Wick."

In a letter to his friend David Bruce, he refers to a sunrise over Wick Bay: "All the seafloor radiates in the glory, and the sky colours melt into whiteness; and over land and sea, rock and cloud, above and around, it is day!"

Who remembers the old "St. Clair" which sailed from Wick to Scrabster? John Horne made three such trips via the Pentland Firth.

He found the viewpoint more than interesting. The white beach at John O'Groats delighted him, but he thought the Stacks of Duncansby were dwarfed from the sea.

The red sandstone of Orkney caught his eye under sunlight and he noted a contrast between Caithness and its northern neighbour.

Impressive is a Keiss memory of John Horne which dates back to his youth, and which he recalled in a letter to his daughter Janey.

"One very fine Sunday we set off (by the sands) to give Mr Scott a hand in his evening service at Keiss Baptist Church – the oldest in Scotland, by the way.

We arrived much too soon. The Sabbath School was about to "skaill". We lay on the roadside facing the sea.

The sun blazed on it like the "sea of glass" in Paradise; everything was still; the scene was altogether idyllic.

As we sat gazing in wonder and admiration at the big ocean, now so quiet, peaceful and immense, the children in the school broke into their closing hymn. It was:

> I will sing you a song of that beautiful land,
>   The far away home of the soul,
> Where the storms never beat on the glittering sand,
>   While the years of eternity roll. etc.
>
> (Sankey 114)

The youthful voices – the sea, sometimes so stormy and wicked – the Calm Shore of the hymn – these seized my imagination with a sudden enthralment of pathos and suggestion that has remained with me (charming me still) to this day."

To return after a year's absence to grass roots was the highlight of the year for this notable Caithnessian who was the guiding hand behind the Calder statue at Wick Riverside, the Tower Memorial at the North Head, and the visitors panel at Station Road, Wick.

John Horne's major literary work is "The County of Caithness" which he edited. Published in 1907, this interesting volume was the standard work on the county for many years, and may be regarded a collector's piece today.

John Horne had a special affection for the Caithness moors and found refreshment of spirit on them. He enjoyed the superb view between Scotscalder and Ben Dorrery when the heather was purple and the sun shone strong on the landscape, and he recorded:

"When you get a good day in Caithness, it's a pearl!"

In the Dorrery letter he praises the view from Ben Dorrery and says: "here, there is nothing between you and the Eternal God".

Northward, he relished the scene from Holborn Head to Dunnet Head – and southward he counted "27 lochs, lochans, and lochagies graced by the sun".

It appeared to him as though "a monster giantess had broken her

The "Aurora" in Keiss Harbour.
Photographed by Dan Mackay.

string of diamonds and had walked off in proud disdain, leaving them lying in artistic irregularity as they fell."

The book includes an outing to Bower via Gersa. John Horne writes of the church ruin at Bower "glorified by a lavish sun" and, en route, of the people in the fields working as though in the grounds of a monastery.

The quiet sunlit day, with its summer haze, revived homely Caithness scenes which gave way to a sea fog as John Horne, his mother and cousin returned to Wick.

Although John Horne settled in Ayr, his heart was always in Caithness, and through books, poems and sketches, he fostered love and loyalty to the homeland. Ill health dogged him most of his life, yet his spirit was brave and his faith strong.

"Round the Old Home" is an easy going book one can dip into. Overall are the picturesque memories it evokes. Anyone with a knowledge or, better still, affection for Caithness, will find it an engaging read.

R.T.
Further reading:
John Horne – His Life and Works – by George Cameron.
Printed by North of Scotland Newspapers, Wick, Caithness.

It has been the longest spell of quiet weather I can remember at this time of year.

The wet weather of early October, combined with slight frosts and lack of wind, led to a rare display of autumn colours. Usually the leaves of the Olrig woods have been burnt brown by salt spray and ripped off long before turning colour – not this year; indeed, the yellows and reds of the beeches have been better than many further south, where unusually severe frost killed the leaves early. Everyone travelling to Dounreay will have admired the trees around Forss.

There have been few occasions in autumn when I've been out across the flow country in conditions of absolute calm. A long morning, running some of the way, walking the rest, crossing some of the remotest areas in the county. Salmon were splashing in the burns near the spawning grounds and the red deer rut was still in progress; the roars of defiant stags could be heard for miles.

Rounding a bend in a shallow burn valley I saw, just 100 yards ahead, the classic view of a fine stag on the skyline, head thrown back, roaring a challenge. A little further on, when crossing to investigate a small cairn on a knoll, the "cairn" took off, revealing itself as a gold eagle. It flew rapidly away, its huge wingspan and "hinged" wingtips clearly distinguishing it from the much smaller buzzard.

Wild geese and whooper swans are everywhere, congregating on lochs in the evening, feeding on stubble during the day. On one quiet morning of dense fog, the woods by Loch Stemster dripping and autumnal, I could hear the calls of hundreds of greying geese and a few whooper swans out on the loch – but could see hardly any!

Another evening, cycling homeward in the dusk between Bridge of Westfield and Loch Calder, a skein of perhaps 100 geese flew right overhead, out over the loch, to drop in ones and threes into growing dark patches on the far side.

Although mornings and evenings are dark, a fine lunch-hour still gives the occasional opportunity to cycle out of site and jog down the coast to eat my sandwiches out on the low cliff-tops in the low sun watching the swell crashing in white, the Sutherland peaks far to the west, Orkney sharp across the dark blue water.

Little spiders on gossamer threads drift across in the gentle breeze, carpeting the fields in silk so that later on they shine like water as the afternoon sun sets. Each spider rides at the end of a thread, flown like a kite, perhaps two metres long. Once I saw them coming in from the seas on an onshore wind – had they blown out from land further along the coast, or had they travelled all the way from Orkney?

Fresh air and exercise provide, alas, little protection against the ravages of Beijing flu, though perhaps being reasonably fit meant that the worst was over after three days. I sit in a chair, looking out through the window across the sunlit county to the sharp skylines of Morven and Scaraben – have I actually managed to run across that ridge?

Never mind a 20 mile walk, I am quite happy to make it once around the garden, watching a goldcrest in the trees and a robin in the bushes. The distant tops of Ben Klibreck and Ben Hope gleam white in the sun; white too is the frost, lingering in the shade. Too cold to stay out in my current state of health!

It looks like a change in the weather; high cloud rapidly coming in from the west, rising south-east wind, falling barometer. By the time I'm back on the bike we'll surely be into our usual run of storms!

Ralph.

A DAY'S WORTH

In the famous "Travels of Marco Polo", the fortunes of his father and uncle are related with oriental picturesqueness. These adventurers had been absent in the radiant East for three years, accumulating (it was reported) great treasure of pearls. When they returned home, however, they were in rags – much to the disappointment of their expectant relatives, some of whom declined to own them. But the passion of the moment quickly subsided when the supposed tramps unseamed their wastrel garments and liberated rivulets of pearls. Rags and pearls! Strange union! But to those who are not impatient, the hidden pearls are in time revealed.

So of ragged, rustic Cattiland. "Not much to be seen here!" snaps the pampered tourist, or the native whose eyes have not been washed at the springs of insight. Ay, but – unseam the rags! The beauties are there, sure enough – beauties of repose, of wide spaces, of daring headlands, of capacious moors, of shy lochans, of wild flowers, of uplifting airs, of languishing twilights.

Reay has received me for my holiday during the last few years, and has behaved handsomely. It is, indeed, an ideal resort.

The bay is a miniature Bay of Naples, saving that instead of raucous streets and wrangling beggars you have unpeopled sands and the welcome of the sea birds. Here I spent the forenoon. Coming to the little swing bridge that crosses Sandside Burn, I sat down on it to rest, my face seaward and my feet swinging free. On my left was the big knoll of Cnocstanger, shouldering the burn; on my right, the benty edge of the golf course. Between, the burn convoyed itself to the sands, spreading out into innumerable draperies of shimmering lace. Three bairns were playing in the spangles of the surf. Each rising wave, curtsying to the sun, showed green in the sunlight. Beyond, the sea was keen blue. In the far distance, the Hoy headland was half-conscious in a bluey-white haze. The composition was ideal.

I became suddenly aware of a feeling that I was looking on a picture which was to become part of myself and ratify my choicest admirations. Who has not at times experienced those anticipated sensations? Sometimes they come as an emotion, when a half-forgotten song is sung. A new meaning flashes out of the familiar words, and the soul is admitted to a secret chamber hitherto unguessed. The jog-trot song has been recreated, and presents itself in fine apparel. And a scene with which we have been intimate from childhood will sometimes leap at us with a singular freshness, and impress us with the suspicion that we have never really seen it before. This happy engagement was now mine. The garrulous little burn, alive with many whispered secrecies; the dots of humanity touching boundlessness in the surf; the calm, imperturbable mien of the sea; the far, visionary suggestion of Hoy; overhead, a flotilla of broken clouds in a blue archipelago (all so familiar) – these now formed a picture so transcendently sweet and simple that I sat there most of the forenoon, encouraging a mood of exceptional luxury.

It was no shadowgraph or painting, but the real thing! I still see it; and shall continue to see it. It is one of the select pictures in the Louvre of my recollections.

THE MAGIC OF CAITHNESS

A visit to the Retreat of the gracious Robert Dick was the satisfaction of the afternoon. This neuk is five miles up the Isauld Burn, and lies slightly beyond the ruined lime-kiln. It is a lovely little spot: rocky juts and miniature shelters, with a boyish waterfall gallivanting through them. In this secluded shelter Dick preserved the rarer ferns and flowers he found during his wanderings. These have now all disappeared, chiefly purloined by envious visitors; but common ferns are still there, and these (with a few fox-gloves and other wild flowers) leave the nursery some of its attractions. Dick's gentle spirit broods here; indeed, I am not sure but it nestles in every such glenlet all over Cattiland. The most precious gift of providence to our loved county was that of this rare soul. How great he was we have not yet guessed.

In the evening I loitered by the roots of Ben Ra. It matters not how often I go to muse on those hills, I always discover some fresh relationships between them and myself. Perhaps it is because I am ever expectant of some new disclosure. How, indeed, can it be otherwise in those acres of primal heatherland, where everything is so aged and is yet being eternally renewed? "We are all lost children of the stars," it has been finely said by a modern poet. I would say in almost the same words, "We are all lost children of the hills." Other venues have allured us and we seldom seeks the hills. Do we know them as teachers, voiceless yet eloquent? Have we discovered their undogmatic infallibility? Do we pause for their benediction, those evangelists of the Higher Significance?

I rested on the eastern side of the Ben till the sun tottered westward and left me in shadow. I was marooned: and I looked on the stretch of further fields in front, tissued in the dallying sunshine. Is there anything on earth, I wonder, so lowly and yet so passionate as this loitering sunset on the landscapes of Cattiland! Daylight does not depart with a brief, formal handshake: it goes away like a lover, with a delayed, oft-repeated farewell, and a sigh.

After my ramble, I returned to my peat-fire at home. I cuddled into a cosy chair and drew to its comfort.

Outside, the light was still idling on the fields, but faintly. It enamelled them with that half-colour shimmer so characteristic of the afterglow of some summer evenings in Cattiland. The haystacks in front were yellowish and pinky in their mixture of stalk and clover. In the window a bright begonia spread itself between me and the dayset, and its petals blushed a softer crimson – a bonnie modest glow, quite ethereal. The patterns of the curtains began to show their white outlines against the shading window; and I was soon conscious of dusk in the room. Pictures and ornaments became illusions. The peat-fire slowed down: fitful little spurts of flame flung streaky gleams on wall and roof – then they retreated into the heart of the fire and I was left with the red sheen of the peat.

And now, the plain and obvious facts of life withdrew; and my mind, unmoored, obeyed every tide. To what unrelated shores do the thoughts journey under the captaincy of such a mood! What swift voyages you make to harbours of reverie beyond unsounded seas! You live and breathe in the past; you dream of eternity, and almost realise it; you feel your relatedness with all the races of mankind; you think of desolate nations, once vital and proud; you visit deserted homes, and try to imagine the destiny of their one-time inmates; you see the hill-folk as breathless figures, moving to their tasks in the mist; you pity the generations who have passed and now lie so silent and excluded by stream and track; you remember with compassion the people who are aged and frail; you pray for the young, who are to inherit the dreams and activities of the world.

As I rose to retire, the last knob of peat darkened and then crumbled to ashes. So ends everything! – palace, hut, sword and plough, fair maid and lover. A trite reflection; yet into every ending is but a transition "into something new and strange". There are no finalities in nature: every process is the preface to another. And there is neither surplusage nor shortage in all her dominion.

John Horne.
"Summer Days in Cattiland".

"Summer Days in Cattiland" (1929) was John Horne's favourite among his own books.

STEPPAN 'E LONG RO'D BACK

"Ochone, ochone, what a melancholy world o' chimney pots!" sadly observed granny, seated by her window as she gazed over the rugged forest of chimney stacks towards the distant, appealing skyline of the Pentland Hills.

I can see her yet as she pensively uttered those revealing words over 50 years ago, when already over her allotted span, slowly shaking her head and patting her aproned lap in emphasis.

Something of the poignancy of her nostalgia touched my youthful imagination as I looked with fresh interest upon her somewhat stern and wrinkled face, while I tried to picture what cherished Caithness memories she would recollect in her quiet hours. Would it be her girlhood days in the lonely croft at Achryrie, amid the heather moors in summer, and the long trek in winter-time to school? Or the hard thrifty struggle in later years to rear her own family at Bardsmirkie, that culminated in roots being pulled up, and Caithness finally abandoned for the call of the south?

I constantly marvelled at granny's sagacious comments on domestic and political affairs, and at her proud bearing as she traversed the city streets arrayed in black dolman and bonnet glinting with countless sequins, conveying an instant impression of someone equal to any occasion or company. Some day, I mused, I would perhaps visit Achryrie myself and try to recapture and absorb the influences that moulded that staunch character, but alas!, a long lifetime elapsed with all its frustrations of time and circumstances before the opportunity arrived.

On a recent sunny day of scudding clouds as I watched from a Caithness window the panorama of spreading fields and scattered croftings that extended out to the broad back of Benachielt, I could distinguish the height of Dempster Hill dominating the horizon some 10 miles away, and realised intently that just beyond lay the remote and deserted clachan of Achryrie. My resolve was definitely made to procrastinate no longer, and as possibilities proved inconvenient, I decided to make the pilgrimage in the old-fashioned but rewarding way of walking – just as granny must have done.

"Och, never fear, ye'll get a lift aal richt" was the optimistic parting advice as I set off from Tormster on an overcast but cheerful day, with an ample lunch package in my pocket, and a few gnawing misgivings in my mind. Within an hour I was passing a number of roadside crofts where the alert "dowgies" ambled out, suspiciously sniffed my trouser legs and retired to squat and watch my progress with puzzled concern – maybe I seemed "round the bend" to them!

Half a century ago, as a "loon", I had been a welcome visitor to one of these crofts but old friends and my own recognition have gone, and soon I was stepping out on the untenanted moorland road. There is something so exhilarating in exploring the ribbon-like road with its fascinating turns and elevations, that when a speeding car overtook me – its occupants evidently wholly intent on their destination – I was quite content to be ignored, while my previous misgivings were being rapidly forgotten.

On approaching an isolated roadside housie, a wifie came out with a rug to shake, and though she never once glanced in my direction the rug got a very thorough shaking! Over in the distance, remote dwellings were identified with pleasure, and became transformed from a mere map-spot to a living abode.

Presently the road entered a large plantation of 20 foot trees that I remembered newly planted out on the vacant moor – it seems but a few years ago. Now what a transformation! It embraces the fascination, the seclusion aye, and the apprehension of a primeval forest that encloses the traveller. On emerging from the woodlands, the way steadily ascended with extending vistas until all Caithness seemed vividly revealed in her appealing majesty, and now I found myself striding out in joyful confidence as the miles disappeared behind me. Surely this was the hard and intimate way our forebears grew to love their land, so difficult for us now in this age of speed.

With high elation I swung down the road past the mystical standing stones, with the blue Scarabens and Morven framed beyond the immense heatherland to the south, and turned up the unfamiliar roadie past Dempster Lochan towards Achryrie. The going at first was excellent, and an adjacent lily-studded tarn quite surprised me. The long tortuous way deteriorated into a neglected track, and I knew I was walking back into history as I carefully picked my steps, and louped over the rough patches towards the old placie.

A throbbing tractor loaded with peats half a mile away changed direction calculated to cross my path, so I discreetly left the track and hailed the driver, introducing myself and my objective. "Weel, weel", was his friendly reply " 'Ere's 'e shepherd up 'ere at 'e merch fence. He'll give ye aal 'e informashan' ye waant, cheerio" and as both the shepherd and I arrived simultaneously at the fence gate, he casually remarked "Ahm chist tyan up 'iss gatie wi' a bittie o' weir. A couple o' sheep hed got through." On reiterating my quest, he confirmed "Weel, boy, yur on 'e richt ro'd then" but after giving directions, decided to accompany me over a short cut until we reached the ridge ahead, and there, a few hundred yards away, was Achryrie.

After a delightful exchange of old-time recollections of places and people, he anxiously enquired "But yur no waalkan' back till Tormster ir ye? Chist ye caal at 'e hoose an' Ah'll run ye in." As we parted I knew the warm value of a couthie Caithness welcome.

With bonnet in hand, I skipped over the tussocky heather to the deserted ruins, and stood for a few minutes in silent contemplation. Resting thankfully upon a massive clump of heather, I relaxed and tried to think back the 120 years to visualise granny as a fresh red-haired lassagie playing or working around those aged walls. And that old gnarled bourtree, too, would likely have been her shelter in storm, and shade in sunshine, while the same scents of the hill still blow.

It seemed appropriate to break bread over here, while my impressions and thoughts bridged well beyond a century and paid homage to granny's memory. After walking round the gaping flagstone fence, I wandered reverently through the grass-grown remains of apartments and animal stalls, and so carried away a fulfilled picture of old Achryrie as I reluctantly returned back the long track to the road, with teeming thoughts thronging my head, and a half peat tucked in my pocket in memento. I felt too transported to trouble the shepherd for his kindly offer, and steadily set off up the empty road ahead. Many times I halted to turn and admire the diminishing and enthralling view until it finally vanished behind me as the roadway turned and dipped over the crest. My steps were not now so swack, and the plantation seemed a long way off, and later appeared much more extensive as I traversed it, though my passage was enlivened by an unexpected sight of the ruddy-brown figure of a disturbed fox scudding away through the undergrowth. A mile further on, a car sped past me, then stopped with open door as I advanced.

"Wid ye lek a lift?" I gratefully accepted and as the driver re-started he commented "Ah'm only goan a mile an' a half" but at that stage we were so "chief" that he continued another mile and a half out of his way. Blessans on ye, boy!

With renewed zest I soon completed my return journey, a little belated, perhaps, but greatly elated at having achieved another Caithness red-letter day.

Perchance when I suddenly behold an expanse of the city's rooftops with its multitude of smoking chimneys, the picture fades, and I am couched again on a clump of Caithness heather, looking through granny's eyes over the wide chequered pattern of moorland, from the village of old Achryrie.

George McLeod.
Reprinted from 1962 issue of Edinburgh Caithness Magazine.

THE GOLDEN CORN

Once again the fields which were "white unto the harvest" are bare, and each farm has its quota of great comfortable looking stacks silhouetted against the skyline. Modern methods and Government subsidies ensure that the farmer, in this atomic age, is not so dependent on a good harvest as were his predecessors at the beginning of the century.

In 1903, my father and his father-in-law took over a 1000 acre farm most of its moorland, and therefore suitable for sheep, at a rent then of £80 the half year, about eight miles inland from the town of Wick in Caithness, putting my uncle Will in as shepherd and manager, for my grandfather had his own farm, and my father had a business in Edinburgh. They had to start from scratch, and looking back at a Record Book of the earliest years, it is amazing what they were able to accomplish with very little money, much wisdom and foresight, and a great deal of hard work.

Most of the stock and implements were purchased at farm sales in various parts of the county, while others were taken over at valuation. One item, "threshing mill valued at £65, catches my eye, and brings back a memory of my early childhood when the corn was gold in the sheaf, and when my brother and I, on holiday, would be thrilled to hear that there would be "threshan e' morn".

In the stackyard, between the farmhouse and the county road, there would be still a quantity of the previous year's corn unthrashed, because the sheaves had been stacked just as they came from the stooks. Also in this stackyard there was a huge mill dam, shallow at one end and quite deep at the other, a wonderful place for ducks and geese. At the deep end there was a sluice.

As children, my brother Frank and I were never allowed to go near the dam by ourselves, neither into the wheelhouse nor near the machinery in the barn, but my father in his wisdom, showed us all those forbidden places and things, and realising the dangers, we were obedient. We were told not to go into the chaff or "caff" house, as part of the machinery was there too, but after all hens nested there and the cats had kittens, so we popped in and out. The chaff, of course, was used as a filling for mattresses, and if feathers were scarce, into pillows and bolsters as well. We were always careful, however, to remove every bit of chaff from our boots and stockings! We played in the strawbarn and we explored the big barn and its lofts.

There was a bruizer, and fanners, and other contraptions of which we did not know the names, brooms, and shovels, and gowpens, empty sacks and sacks of coom, and bran, and bruised corn. There would be great slabs of "oilcake", and sometimes bags of feeding stuffs with bits of what we called "locust" beans, which we chewed. We tasted the oilcake too, but didn't think much of it!

We would go up the wide open plain wooden stair hanging with lacy cobwebs misted with meal dust, peep sideways at a window obscured with more webs, where great fat lively spiders pounced on unwary bluebottles, flies and moths. After their struggles they too were "dressed in meal dust", giving added protein, no doubt. If a great brute of a rat passed us on the stair we were not unduly perturbed. He knew as well as we did, that one room upstairs was the granary, and that corn would be lying inches deep on the floor. Young as we were, we never played amongst it, nor walked on it, for we knew that this was part of "our daily bread".

The barn had a smell of its own. It clung to the stone walls, and to the flagstone floor, it hung from the rafters, and it was in the air; unforgettable and indescribable – an aroma, praise be, which changes not with time, nor with the barn's disuse.

Before the day of the threshing, certain arrangements had to be made

The waning year has its own attractions: the fields have yielded their harvest, and now stand mellow under the autumn sun. The homesteads share in this seasonal picture. . .

Illustration by Alan Thomson.

regarding extra labour etc. Already a cartload or two of sheaves had been taken down from the stackyard and halted under the high wooden door of the loft, where the sheaves were to be fed into the mill. A man on top of the cart would pitchfork the sheaves through the open door, and the person receiving them would stack them against a wall. The remainder would be brought next day while the mill was in operation. It had to be a good day or the event would be postponed, so we all hoped and prayed it would be fine.

Tomorrow eventually became today, and soon everyone was at his post, two to unloose the straw bands or cut the binder twine, one to feed each loosened sheaf into the mill, two downstairs in the barn to fill the empty sacks with grain as it came swiftly down the narrow wooden chute, remove a full sack quickly, whip under an empty one, have the full one tied with twine, the foot of the "hurley" pushed under the full sack and hauled over the flagstone floor to the other end of the barn.

The cats had made a hurried departure from the chaff house, and the rats had disappeared, but a few hens, disturbed from their usual nesting place in the strawbarn, half flew, half ran out at the door, in a flurry of feathers and squawking furiously, making the first few discordant notes of the day.

Once the stage was set, the signal would be given, and someone would run up to the stackyard and open the sluice. The water suddenly released, ran down under the road, passing the workshop and the stable, and then under the flagstone floor of the strawbarn, along the wide wooden platform overhanging, or partially overhanging, the huge water wheel. Slowly and uncertainly at first, the wheel moved round and round, and then, as it gathered momentum, the whole complicated machinery of the threshing mill was set in motion.

The shuddering noise was fantastic and exciting. Miscellaneous sounds of splashing and tumbling of water, the slapping sounds of leather belts revolving around steel, the shirring sound of corn grains in their thousands sliding down the wooden chute, the soft patter of chaff falling like snowflakes into the "caff-house", and the rustle of straw as it tumbled down, a curtain of golden rain, into the strawbarn, were pleasing to the ear.

Outside there was the occasional clip-clop of the horses' hooves, and the rumble of the cart wheels, as more sheaves were brought from the stackyard.

People shouted to each other above the noise, the cobwebs shook in the window, and the old wood stair vibrated under our feet as we went down to see the filling of the sacks with grain.

We knew that some of it would be sent to the meal mill at Lyth, that the adults would speak of "sids" and sowans", but we knew that new oatmeal would come back to help fill the girnel for another year. Oatmeal for brose, for porridge, for oatcakes, for spooning over thick sour milk, or if you were lucky, on cream out of the "kirn" for coating herrings fresh from the sea, for "skirley", for stuffing (along with fat and onions, pepper and salt) for a big fat hen, for "cropin heid" (before my time!) – stuffed cod's head which was said to look like a fat French frog. Oatmeal for mealy puddings when the pig was killed, oatmeal for gruel to cure a cough or cold, flavoured of course, with a good splash of whisky! Oatmeal and water to cool one's hands before "clapping" the butter, and oatmeal and sugar for the bairns instead of a sweetie.

Too soon for us, the threshing would be over. The supply of water would be cut off, and slowly, with a diminution of all sounds in reverse, the whole magic orchestra would come to a stop.

Times change. Today the farm is in other hands. The dam has been drained dry, and a more modern method of threshing the corn is employed, and there have been other changes. But the seasons change not, and every year, in some of those selfsame fields beyond the farmhouse and the steading, with its feet anchored in the good earth, and its head of grain rustling and swaying in the wind, there is yet another harvest of golden corn.

Jane Thomson Langwill.

THE MOORS OF CAITHNESS
*A Song

It is long since I left my native land,
Where all my forebears lie,
Where the wind blows keen o'er vacant moors,
Beneath the dome of sky.
But I shall never forget that land,
Nor the feel of the sun and the rain,
Nor the mile upon mile of heather in bloom,
Across the treeless plain.

I still can see the gleaming snow
With its mantle over all,
And I still can hear the drumming snipe
And the curlew's haunting call.
That call will always summon me
Wherever I may roam,
And bring to mind the kindly years
At Halsary, my home.

The salmon will run by Cattag Stream
On their journey from the sea,
The swan and the wild goose will take their rest
Beside Ben Alisky.
And I like them will come again,
No matter where I be,
For Morven, the Pap, and the Scaraben
Have put their spell on me.

Though time and age may make me frail,
That spell will hold me fast,
And bring me thoughts of peace and quiet
And comfort at the last.
Though my bones will lie in the city's smoke
Beside those loved by me,
My spirit will wander the Caithness moors,
Till all eternity.

George Mowat

**Words and music by the late George Mowat;
arranged by Miss Martha Smith.*

BIRTHDAY POEM
For My Twin Brother Alan in 1985

Sunset steals across the sky
   Its magic wand aglow
And o'er Dunnet Sands
   The light of day expires,
A red-gold path
   Rests upon the Pentland sea,
We knew in days lang syne.

Swift-winged memories return
   With the gulls haunting cry
Sunlit days of yore
   That hold a testament of youth
Beyond the rainbow's end:
   O for those glorious days
In the land of Tir-nan-og [1]

Ronald Thomson.

[1] "Land of the ever young"

There is a memorial seat to Alan in the grounds of Caithness General Hospital.

Alan & Ronald Thomson, Quintfall Farm, Lyth, Caithness (1951).
Photographed by Jane Thomson Langwill.

A DAY OF EXTREMES

It had been some day – and it wasn't over yet! But the best laid plans of mice and men, as they say, gang aft agley.

We had disembarked from the early-morning train after lodging a special request to stop at lonely Altnabreac. It was a quarter to seven in the morning. And it felt awfully remote.

In the lee of the nearby Lochdhu Hotel, an imposing former shooting lodge and one-time hostelry – long since closed – we hurriedly changed into waterproof clothing. A torrential squall hosed down on the vast landscape that opened up before our eyes. It was utterly bare and empty. And we were all alone and at the mercy of the elements.

The forecast was not good and we had come prepared to expect the unexpected.

At Dalnawillan, after a four-mile trek across exposed tracks, we intended to cross the river by means of an ageing, rickety, swing bridge Many foot-planks, we knew from previous experience, had either rotted or broken away.

But the Glutt Water was living up to its name. Floods of spate river powered by in front of us, dragging what little was left of our only link with Ben Alisky. Two wires reached over, loosely, to stanchions rooted on the opposite riverbank but neither I nor Dave, my walking companion, seriously considered the commando option!

There was no hope of fording the swollen river and our plans to scale Ben Alisky and then to strike out for Dunbeath and the shelter of its seven-mile strath had clearly been dashed.

Our destination, reached alternatively by traversing estate roads via Dalganachan, Glutt Lodge and Braemore, lay a seemingly endless 16 miles away. With weather conditions worsening, there was little to debate so we headed off across the bleak tracks.

The school bus, with only one passenger on board, pulled away as we drew close to Dalganachan, an isolated estate worker's house – and the home, apparently, of Caithness's remotest pupil. The nearest primary school in Halkirk is 16 miles in the opposite direction (Altnabreac school having closed a few years ago when its school roll fell to an "unviable" level).

Sunlight and snow. Caithness is renowned for its very own climatic qualities. Talk about all the seasons in one day! But this was a day of extremes.

Near-monsoon downpours succumbed to hurricane-force winds, in turn relenting, strangely, to silent fluffy snow falls.

The lighting conditions were equally variable – searing sun-rays one minute bursting through an interminable grey void only to disappear the next, smothered by an oppressive purple-blackness. Behind us we sensed just such an imminent black force. It seemed almost malevolent. "This one's going to be the mother and the father," Dave's tone was loaded and anxious. "We need to shelter quickly."

But where, in this vast emptiness?

And then, as if on cue, we breasted a rise in the track and in the dip below a small brig spanned an upper feeder stream of the Dunbeath water – and beside it a corrugated garage!

"We can shelter in the lee side," I suggested.

On further investigation, we discovered the doors were not padlocked. Sliding back the bolt, to escape the tempest, we ventured inside and there, incredibly, was an antique padded armchair. . .

Outside, mother and father were engaged in a screaming match. But safely inside, the corrugated garage, with its antique padded armchair, offered a welcome respite.

After the storm we ventured out, entrusting ourselves once more to the elements. Braemore, and the road-end telephone kiosk which would summon assistance, was another four miles away.

Morven towered to our immediate right – a massive conical sentinel protecting the county's southern flanks.

Strange intermittent lighting conditions played tricks with the Maiden Pap, whose partially snow-covered braes glittered fleetingly, like a sequinned gown.

At her feet the "little loch of the brindled cow" – Lochan nam Bo Riabhach – boiled over like bubbling mercury as laser-like sunbeams splashed molten cascades in the stiff westerly breeze.

And then, at last, the lost glen: Braemore, the only truly "Highland" locality in Caithness. Surrounded by a sea of reliefless moorland, Braemore evokes that self-same aura only previously found on the island of Stroma. A tangible atmosphere tinged with sadness for the lost communities of times gone by. A paradise lost. . .

Dave drew heavily on the stiff, creaking hinges of the telephone kiosk. He would summon a car to transport us back to reality. But he reappeared almost immediately, asking, "What's the code for Lybster?".

He seemed oddly out of touch – almost bewildered. It had been that kind of day.

Dan Mackay,
John O'Groat Journal.

SNOWSTORM

Dawn was breaking one Sunday morning in January almost 50 years ago, when I got out my bicycle to cycle the three miles to pick up my lift to work. It had all the appearance of being a crisp, clear and cold winter's day. On arrival in Castletown, I left my bicycle in its usual place at the end of a house. No need to worry about it being stolen in those days. My conveyance duly arrived and we set out for Skitten Airfield a few miles outside Wick. Johnny, at that time, was one of my superiors and he was fortunate to be the possessor of a car and perhaps more importantly he was able to obtain petrol to run it.

It was our custom in those wartime days to work seven days a week and all sorts of hours. Sunday was generally spent clearing up all the sundry bits of paperwork which had accumulated during the rest of the week.

We duly arrived at Skitten and by this time it was a beautiful winter's morning – the like of which you can only get in Caithness – not for long. We soon realised that the sky was darkening and the wind was beginning to rise. A hint of snow as a few flakes began to fall. We decided to make a cup of tea and see how things looked after that. Now it was really snowing and the wind was howling. Decision time – we would head for home. A quick tidy up and having locked the office we got into the car and set off across the airfield. At the end of a hangar we ran into a snowdrift. Having dug the car out we set off again, but not for long. This time we were well and truly stuck. It was obvious that Johnny's little Ford eight or whatever, was never going to make the exit from the Airfield on to the main road, far less Castletown. Help was at hand however, or so we thought. A couple of R.A.F. lads helped to free us from the snowdrift and suggested that we leave the car in a hangar on the Airfield and they would give us a run along the road in one of their trucks. So far, so good. However, half a mile along the road the truck came to an abrupt halt. By this time it was an absolute raging blizzard. Regrettably, they said, "sorry, we cannot go any further".

What to do now. There was no way we could contact our homes, so we decided to walk. I should mention that we had no office safes in those days and it was the custom of whoever was locking up at night to take the cash box and any money home with them. The cash box had been in the boot of Johnny's car and we had taken it with us when we got into the R.A.F. truck. It must have been full of nothing but coins because it was a dead weight. I learned afterwards that there was about £100 of silver in it!!

Anyway we set out. The road was getting pretty full with the snow blowing off the fields. We struggled through huge drifts. Our guide was the telegraph poles, when we could see them. We had tied a piece of string to each other so that we could at least keep together, and all the time there was this box. As I recall, a soldier caught up with us. He was attempting to walk to Thurso. I don't remember whether he was going on leave or coming back, but being from the South of England he certainly did not think much of Caithness weather. However, being much fitter than us, he soon left us behind. Johnny and I trudged on and on. We were soaking wet and the icicles were forming on hair, eyebrows etc. It did not seem to matter. The cash box – we should have tossed it away into the snow. After several hours we came to an army camp and we staggered into the nearest hut where we gratefully accepted a mug of steaming hot tea from the soldiers. Somewhat refreshed, we set out again. Eventually, Castletown, Johnny was almost home. I had another few miles to go. No point in looking for the bicycle. Take the road over Birklehill. Weary and 'soakan weet', home at last.

In those days we did not boast hot water or a bath and so it was a case of getting dried the best way one could. A plate of my mother's 'tattie soup', which was always part of Sunday's dinner and one began to thaw out and feel better.

A good night's sleep and back to normal. Next morning Caithness was a white wilderness. The wind had gone down, the sky was bright and clear and the sun was shining.

When we meet, Johnny and I often recall that Sunday, 50 years ago. It never occurred to us that we would not make it. We could, I am sure, have obtained shelter for the night at any of the cottages along the way from Skitten to Castletown but the thought never crossed our minds. Today I suppose we would have been classed as foolhardy, thoughtless, stupid, etc. Well, perhaps, were we?

John Lockie – Edinburgh Caithness Magazine.

Men have lived here for thousands of years; the chambered cairns erected 5,000 years ago are still there, the brochs and castles, sites of war and battle, are everywhere.

Standing stones and stone circles and stone rows are so common as to be overgrown and unvisited. Yet man has made little real impact on the county, save perhaps by the recent devastating plantations on large areas of the flow country.

Caithness is the county of the cliffs and the moors, the great seabird colonies, the sanctuaries for flora and fauna on the steep broken slopes of the east coast, blue butterflies over banks of flowers. It is that great sense of space, emptiness and light of the flow country, the dark-blue water of a remote loch rippling on to sand. It is the wail of the red-throated diver, the mournful golden plover, the musical greenshank. It is the utter silence of the Knockfin Heights under deep January snow.

Caithness is the wind, never still, fresh summer breezes, 100mph squalls of hail blasting in on a January night, semi-liquid with mist and drizzle for days on end in July. It is the mud and darkness and storms of December. It is the absolute clarity of air on a May evening, skylines sharp as far as Birsay, Morven, Foinaven and Cape Wrath.

It is the welcome evening sea-breeze after a rare hot summer day, it is the whiteout blizzard and blocked roads with a complete thaw three days later. It is all four seasons in a day, any time of the year, and the weather-forecaster's despair.

Caithness is the people. It is the place. It is much more than both.

Ralph, Caithness Courier.

The custom of "resting" a peat fire used to be commonplace in Caithness – those were the days when all cooking, baking and heating of water, was done over an open fire. Thus the fire was seldom allowed to die out and last thing at night a large flat peat or "boorag" was laid upon the embers to smoulder till morning.

PEAT SMOORAN' PRAYER

Oh Lord, we thank thee for the peats
    We garner from the hill
We thank thee for their heat and light;
    Thy grace be with us still.

And when those large brown peats
    Upon the embers red;
Keep thou their spark of life intact
    While we sleep safe in bed.

And when the morning light appears
    A cheerful flame we ask;
That man and bairn may have their meat,
    Before the daily task.

And Lord, if one should die tonight,
    And leave this earthly land;
Take thou the embers of that life,
    And "rest" them in thy hand.

Jane Thomson Langwill.

THE MAGIC OF CAITHNESS

Memorials come in all forms but the one I am thinking of is a Christmas tree at Corsback in the Parish of Dunnet.

I bought the tree in Thurso and took it home where it had pride of place over the Festive season.

Christmas trees are usually discarded after New Year – but not this one – for mother planted it in the garden. The tree had seemed too nice to throw away.

The tree had no roots, and few might have expected it to survive, but surprisingly it did. It has grown and thrived for more than 30 years and in a land scarce of trees become more precious.

After mother's death, the idea of a Caithness memorial was suggested but not realised. Yet there in Caithness **was** a memorial in front of our former home, one which had been planted with hope in the dead of winter.

True there is no name affixed to the tree, but some memorials go beyond words, and the fact they exist is what matters. And what they symbolise.

Such is the memorial at Corsback – a living memorial to a gracious lady who loved Caithness – Jane Thomson Langwill (1902-78).

MAGIC CIRCLE

Brooding clouds eclipse the sun
   And drift across the sky,
The ground is bone hard
   Unyielding as a miser;
The day is stone cold
   Save for the magic circle
Of our winter fire;
   The unclothed trees, stark,
Hold their January vigil.

Marauding winds and sunless sky
   Landscape bleached of colour,
Only the potency of memory
   Subtracts the winter day
Into the loveliness of summer.

Ronald Thomson.

At a glance Kenn can take in the whole steel-shimmering triangle of the Moray Firth. Each of its sides is barely 70 miles. For its size it is one of the finest breeding grounds of fish – and perhaps of men – to be found in any firth of the seven seas. Since the birth of his grandfather, its story to Kenn is intricate with the doings of men and women, legendary or known to him. The rocks are quiet enough today. Even the headlands are stretched out in sleep. But Kenn smiles, knowing the rocks and the headlands, and that innocent shimmer of the quiet water like a virgin shield!

As he wheels slowly, the great plain of Caithness opens before his eyes and the smile that had been in them deepens with affection. This is the northland, the land of exquisite light. Lochs and earth and sea pass away to a remote horizon where a sauve of pastel foothills cannot be anything but cloud. Here the actual picture is like a picture in a supernatural mind and comes upon the human eye with the surprise that delights and transcends memory. Gradually the stillness of the far prospect grows unearthly. Light is silence. And nothing listens where all is of eternity.

Pride quickens the smile. This bare, grim, austere Caithness treeless, windswept, rock-bound, hammered by the sea, hammered, too, by successive races of men, broch-builders and sea-rovers, Pict and Viking. Against the light, Kenn veils his eyes and wheeling round sees the Orkneys anchored in the blue seas with the watermark of white on their bows. Brave islands, he feels like saluting them with a shout.

Westward yet, and the granite peaks of Ben Laoghal, the magic mountain, beckons towards Cape Wrath and the Arctic. Westward still, and all the dark mountains of Sutherland march on Ben Mor Assynt, beyond which is the Atlantic and the Isles of the west.

Kenn completes the circle and his vision narrows on the winding strath beneath him, upon its skyey thread of water that links mountain to sea, west to east; the strath where all he has seen is given living shape and desire; and suddenly closing his wings, he stoops upon the moving figure on the river bank.

But the small figure does not hear the singing ecstasy in the wings; has no knowledge of the eyes that presently peer at him, noting with scientific care every breath of expression, each detail of the face, the dark hair cut across the forehead, the long thin hands and thin wrists, the bare legs and feet. The eyes are hazel brown, with flecks in them, and – this is surprising but instantly right – full of a glancing light of apprehension.

For Kenn had forgotten the fear, the wonder, the sudden heartbeat, the strangeness, the sense of adventure, the ominous quality in known things when encountered in lonely places. He had thought it more carefree and golden, more reckless and laughing and thoughtless.

This young figure is not only intensely but mysteriously preoccupied. For one whole half minute he stands staring at the tip of a drooping twig which his finger nails tear bit by bit. Slowly he turns his head to one side with an odd self-conscious expression, as if expecting someone to come round the corner of the bank.

Is he carrying on a conversation with Beel? Is he the hero in an imaginary poaching raid? What makes the skin – so smooth, so tender – seem suddenly to darken shyly, as if thought had been overhead? The

THE MAGIC OF CAITHNESS

lips part as he listens. Something fainter than a smile quivers in his lashes, and the half minute ends in a quick stepping away.

Kenn watches and follows him, and finds him resting in the shelter of some trees near the Lodge Pool. He is excited now lest he be seen. He has never been so far up the river before. Tentatively he steps out on the smooth green bank to look at the pool.

Kenn waits in the trees watching him with profound attention for the little figure out there is himself.

Neil M. Gunn
(Highland River).

SUNSET

Sometimes a few lines of verse can reflect the essence of Caithness, more evocatively than a page of prose.

"O to be back where the peewits are crying
Back where the gowans spread over the lea,
Back where the wind through the heather is sighing,
And sweet lilting burnies dance to the sea" *.

Caithness is an amalgam of many things to be enjoyed. Without doubt she has havens of quiet to delight the visitor, and after the hurly-burly of city life what could be better? The relaxed tempo of country life is the best antidote to stress, and Caithness offers peace in plenty.

There is a stillness at dayset which is especially pleasing. Imagine a day of strong wind has ceased, there is a timeless serenity in the air, it is a period for reflection. Perhaps there may be a sunset to mark the ending of the day.

Northern sunsets are justly notable but one was superlative: it was an August evening on the Thurso to Castletown road, picture a sunset which encircled the sky with a beauty which held one in its wonder; the colour and stillness graced the land and sea like a benediction. A precious experience to witness the glory of such a sunset.

There can of course be a sweet-sadness when sunset comes: "All too soon would come the gloaming, that lovely part of a long summer day, and we would reluctantly wend our way homewards. While the red sun was setting behind the plantation at Barrock, Lyth, a ghostly mist was rising on both sides of the burn and from beyond that grey curtain came the bleat of a sheep or the lonely cry of a bird, or maybe the "goback, goback" of the red grouse, as if he fain would turn back the dark rolling clouds of night." [1]

It takes time to get the best from Caithness. Patience is the keynote, for this northern county has a charm worth discovering, even the changing light offers new impressions to intrigue – and delight. The chaste glories do not, of course, appeal to everyone: too bleak, too monotonous for some, yet Caithness has a quality which still enthralls.

Historian Rosalind Mitchison, paid this tribute: "This is a land of great winds and vast skies; its bare and treeless lines march unencumbered to meet the peculiar width and light of the northern sky. It carries with it a certain dry beauty, which can win affection and make all other landscapes strangely soft." [2]

Dare one hope that some of you who have never visited the county, may feel the urge to discover Caithness for yourself? May those who do have a happy and rewarding time with all the delight new impressions can bright. A safe journey whenever, and wherever, you travel in that enchanted land – Caithness.

[*] "Retrospect" by Duncan B. Sutherland.
[1] Jane Thomson Langwill: "Green Corn".
[2] Rosalind Mitchison: "Agricultural Sir John".

> Yet here the rivulet of life
> Sprang trembling to its conscious dreams;
> And here arose those suns that change
> Its rougher tracks to shining streams.

John Horne.

Could it really be more than 35 years since we lived in Caithness? The thought crossed my mind as I drove along the John O'Groats – Castletown road one summer night of brilliant sunshine – the kind of night which reveals Caithness at her most impressive.

Was it the light or something else which gave the impression that all those years were but one day in the time equation? So many years distilled in the glory of the night, along that road bordered by the Pentland Firth, with Stroma and Orkney, on that northern seascape.

Freedom, renewal of spirit, kinship, a return to grass roots – and in the least expected moments, the Magic of Caithness!

Such allurements draw one back to that land beyond the Ord – neither Highland or Lowland – but undeniably Caithness!

Deo Gratias.

Ronald Thomson.

ONCE AGAIN

I've heard again the skylark sing
Athwart the morning cloud,
And blissful stood beneath his wing
With pulses thrumming loud!

I've trod again the healing hills
Atop the moorlands wide,
And strayed adown the soothing rills
That through the mosses glide!

I've seen again the sea-gulls wheel
Ayont the rocks of grey,
And gladsome watch'd their buoyant reel
Amid the billows' spray!

I've stood again with bounding heart
Aneath my father's roof
And felt the fret of life depart
Before its calm reproof!

I've knelt again with straining breast
Anear a quiet mound:
And crooned the names of those who rest
Within the holy ground!

****

Now, dusty street for heathy sod;
For sky, the city stain;
But, sacred sights of home-thank God,
I've seen ye once again!

John Horne.

John Horne.

CAITHNESS

Land of riven cliff
  And windblown sea,
Where the winding road
  Lures the eye to wander
Across the face of time,
  Where sun showers magic
On the tumbling river
  And incense of heather
Is potent as wine,
  Where the open sky
Reveals a vast splendour
  From Ord to Dunnet Head.

Again the resplendent sea
  Touches the soul anew,
While the sunlit gull
  Gleans translucent water,
With an old world cry.

Ronald Thomson.

Sunset – Loch Watten.   Photographed by Dan Mackay.

THE MAGIC OF CAITHNESS

RECOMMENDED BOOKS

Calder's History of Caithness – single volume. First published in 1861 – 2nd Edition 1887. History from 10th Century – interesting without being over scholarly makes this readable and authoritative.

Summer Days in Cattiland – John Horne – 1929. Small in size yet rich in content. Interesting aspects by the most popular Caithness writer of his time. A collector's piece.

Round the Old Home – Letters and Speeches by John Horne – Memorial book edited by his daughter, Janey Horne Robertson (1935) – evocative memories of the Far North.

Portrait of Caithness and Sutherland by James Miller, published by Robert Hale, London 1985. The best book of its kind for general readers. Detailed and well written.

Caithness 1925-6. Excellent picture-book rich in nostalgia by Herbert Sinclair. Another collector's piece – especially for Caithness exiles.

Caithness Your Home – Herbert Sinclair (1930) Companion book to Caithness 1925-6. Print quality reproduction better, albeit with smaller photographs – nostalgia rating 10 out of 10.

Sun Circle – Neil M. Gunn (1933). A Viking invasion on the Dunbeath Coast, evolves into a major novel – well written and structured, a classic of its kind.

Highland River – Neil M. Gunn (1937). An award winning novel, which gave its author the impetus to become a full-time writer. This novel, set in his native Dunbeath, has an evergreen quality.

Times Gone By – Volume One. Excellent reminders of the special Christmas John O'Groat Journals which appeared between 1923-1937. Selected by Clive Richards and published in 1991 by North of Scotland Newspapers.

The Gardens of Queen Elizabeth, the Queen Mother: A Personal Tour with the Marchioness of Salisbury. Published by Penguin Books Limited in 1988. Not a Caithness book, but worthy of inclusion because of its excellent chapter on the Castle of Mey Gardens with superb colour photography by Derry Moore. A classic book of its kind.

MAGIC OF CAITHNESS

A Northern Outlook – Donald Omand – published by North of Scotland Newspapers. Attractively written essays which first appeared in the John O'Groat Journal and Caithness Courier between 1957-1987. Much to stir the memory of the most seasoned reader – illustrated with black and white photographs (1991).

Valley of Wild Birches – Arthur Ball – 1994. The Barrock poet's retrospective collection includes some poems of Caithness interest which are among his best work. Printed by North of Scotland Newspapers, this was Arthur Ball's last poetry book – he died in December 1994. A nice reminder of his talent.

The Silver Darlings – Neil M. Gunn – 1941. The Dunbeath novelist's most popular book: "A story of epic proportions concerning the herring fishing in the early 19th Century. Described by one critic as the finest balance of metaphysical speculation and concrete epic making that any fiction writer in English has achieved this century". – Dairmid Gunn. (Published by Faber & Faber).

The County of Caithness – Edited by John Horne – Published by W. Rae, Wick, in 1907. This comprehensive volume was for many years the standard reference book, and even today contains much to interest the Caithness student.

Caithness From the Air – The superb colour photography of George Robb, plus the novelty factor, make this publication, by North of Scotland Newspapers, a welcome presentation indeed.

THE MAGIC OF CAITHNESS

SIX FAVOURITE VIEWS

Sunset over Dunnet Head.
Sinclair Bay from the Braehead at Keiss.
Wick Bay from the North Head.
Watten Loch at sunset.
Thurso Bay from Holborn Head.
Seaview from the Latheron coast.

SIX FAVOURITE LOCALES

Forss Falls.
Wick Riverside.
Berriedale Cove.
Thurso Riverside.
Dirlot.
Dunbeath Strath.

SIX CAITHNESS MEMORIES

Summer holidays at Quintfall Farm, Lyth.
Seeing the "Northern Lights" from Corsback, Dunnet.
Cutting peat on Dunnet Head.
My first visit to the Cross at Altimarlach.
The Royal Yacht Britannia in Thurso Bay.
Our debut visit to Langwell Gardens.

The Queen Mother pictured in the grounds of The Castle of Mey.
Photographed by John Adams.

ACKNOWLEDGEMENTS

I wish to thank H.M. Queen Elizabeth, the Queen Mother, for allowing a private visit to the gardens and grounds of the Castle of Mey in connection with this book.

I am also grateful to Dairmid Gunn for his welcome foreword to the Magic of Caithness, also for permission to include the writings of Neil M. Gunn (Alasdair and Dairmid Gunn are copyright holders of the Gunn literary estate). To Jessie G. McLeod for her poem Catanasia; to Messrs Cassels, London, for a quotation from Winston S. Churchill's "A History of the English Speaking Peoples" (Volume I); to Ralph for Caithness Courier writings; S. Miller Gault for his Lybster Train memories; Maureen Nugent for her poem Memory Pictures; Janet Mackay for her Lybster article; Arthur Ball, Barrock, for his poetry; Elizabeth Jack for her Wick Pre 1914 memoir; Jessie Stewart for her Peace poem; Margaret Aitken for her Stroma article; Isabel Richardson for her Flagstones poem; Elizabeth McArdle for her poem, Walk in Caithness; Dan Mackay for his Flow Country article; The Sunday Telegraph, London for a quotation from Gwen Moffat's article, Life at the Top; Rev E. Horstman's Caithness article; Margaret Woodhouse for the writings of John Horne; John Lockie for his Snowstorm article; Nancy Roloff's, Favourite Caithness View article; memoirs of John Herries McCulloch which first appeared in the Daily Express; W. A. Mackay for "Scarborough Jimmy"; to Alexandrina MacGregor for her Wick memoirs from A. Chapbook of Wick, Caithness; to Florence E. Wymans for her Scrabster tribute. I also acknowledge the writings of George and Ada B. McLeod, Malcolm Mackenzie and George Mowat; Caithness historian James T. Calder deserves credit too.

Donald Mackay, Henry Henderson (Bard of Reay) and Alexander Miller's poetry are acknowledged from Caithness Notebooks, published by John Humphries, Thurso.

I acknowledge my late mother, Jane Thomson Langwill's writing; also my twin brother, Alan Thomson's work in this anthology. The Time Magazine article, "Navigation, Magical Stones of the Sun", previously appeared in our "Whispering Winds" anthology.

I am grateful to Dan Mackay for his landscape photographs, and for taking extra pictures for this book; to John Humphries for the Bard of Reay illustration; to Mario Luciani for the Neil Gunn photograph; to my brother Gordon Thomson, for the Corsback photo of Alan and Ronald Thomson; the Vintage Pictures of Caithness by my mother Jane; also Jack Sinclair's drawing of Bridge Street, Wick. I acknowledge the harvest drawing by my twin brother, Alan. The picture of John Horne was taken from Round The Old Home and the end piece drawing is from Lifeline Magazine.

I record thanks to Clive Richards, Commercial Manager, of North of Scotland Newpapers, for deciding to publish this Caithness anthology. Also to Alan Hendry, Editor of Groat and Courier, my thanks.

I owe special thanks to Mandy Brown, for her work as typist and proof reader, on The Magic of Caithness. Her co-operation is much appreciated.

To all those in Caithness who have shown friendship and hospitality – over many years – may this book be a symbol of thanks and remembrance.

Ronald Thomson.

END PIECE

The Magic of Caithness is a nostalgic reminder of Scotland's Far North, that land of the big sky, moorland wilderness, and dramatic coastline. Familiar names like Neil Gunn, John Horne, plus other writers reveal a composite picture from Berriedale to Reay, in this illustrated anthology edited by Ronald Thomson.

A former editor of the Edinburgh Caithness Magazine, Ronald finds most of the inspiration for his writing comes from the Far North. His work has appeared in the Scots Magazine, the John O'Groat Journal, the Caithness Courier, Lifeline Magazine, Israel Today, the Lady Magazine, the Edinburgh Evening News and the Edinburgh Caithness Magazine.

This anthology will be of special interest to anyone who knows Caithness, or better still has an affection for Scotland's most northern county on the mainland.

The Portland Arms Hotel

UNDER THE PERSONAL SUPERVISION OF THE PROPRIETORS:
HELEN & GERALD HENDERSON

LYBSTER, CAITHNESS KW3 6BS.
Telephone (01593) 721208   Fax. 721446

The Family run Hotel with a traditional friendly welcome and a range of top quality modern services.

Staying at The Portland Arms Hotel is guaranteed to be a unique experience in terms of friendly service, high standards of accommodation and top quality food, beautifully prepared for your pleasure.

Eating at The Portland Arms is a very popular and special event in Caithness. The variety and quality of dishes is renowned and the 'never ending' sweet trolley considered a tremendous bonus to end a perfect meal.

Local fresh produce, including beef, game (in season), fish, seafood and vegetables provide the majority of ingredients on the menu beside other quality foods such as succulent Aberdeen Angus steaks.

MEMBER

Scottish TOURIST BOARD COMMENDED

AA

RAC
★ ★ ★

FAMOUS FOR ITS CUISINE, THE PORTLAND ARMS OFFERS TRADITIONAL SUNDAY LUNCHES, HIGH TEAS & DINNERS SERVED DAILY AND BAR SUPPERS DAILY BETWEEN 5 & 9 p.m.

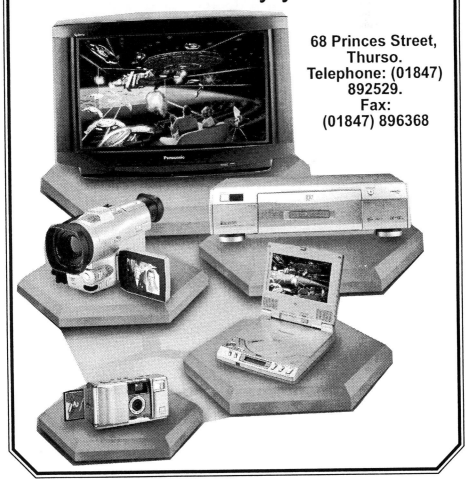

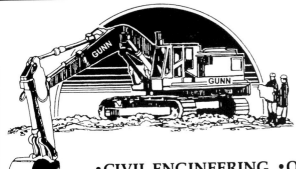

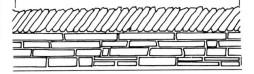

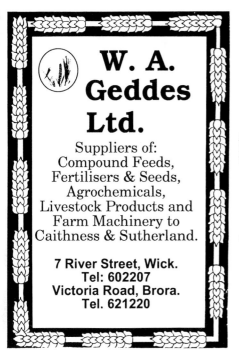